Man Hate

Marcy Allen B.S.

DEDICATION

To the Manosphere and the Red Pill junkies with love because love is all that matters.

For my beautiful daughter without whom I would know little about love. I thought I would be a cat lady by now.

For my Mom and Dad.

For A.C. who is one of the best people I've ever met.

CONTENTS

ACKNOWLEDGMENTS

I am so grateful for the technology that makes the voice of one person able to be published and pushed out into the world. I am humbled before this power. I am lucky to have some great people in my life that actually love me. Its nuts. They are in no way responsible for this mess.

1 INTRODUCTION

It seems obvious but I guess I need to say it is not ok to do the following to boys: hit them, ridicule them for crying, use them for their money, allow "boys will be boys" as an excuse for hurting anyone, let men get away with not contributing – if you don't bring a dish to pass – you don't get to eat, assume and tolerate violence from boys, not teach them how to take care of themselves and others or allow them to treat woman as parts instead of people.

No one wants to hear me complain about rape. Be happy someone is interested in my body right? It is sad that they had to do what they did to me. Why did they feel they had to? What the hell? Why do men hate women? Have we raped you? Almost never! Is it because we take your jobs and do them cheaper? Is it because you don't take responsibility for yourself in any measurable way?

Maybe I'm approaching things the wrong way but, I'm hoping that if we start treating men more like humans, then men will start treating men more like humans then they will do the same for women. We all want the same things, respect, to be needed and sex. Why can't we figure this out? I hope to make the case here for reason and love instead of the piling on of hate that has sold books on this topic so far. You can't just look at half of a population and expect to come to meaningful conclusions. There is so much money in keeping us sick and fighting with each other, it's time that we try something else.

Vocabulary that I had to look up: Misogyny- the hatred or dislike of women or girls. Misogyny can be manifested in many ways including sexual discrimination, denigration of women, violence against women and sexual objectification of women. Wikipedia 12-24-2014 I know I am not supposed to use them as a reference but I like them and I give them money. Misandry - the hatred or dislike of men (examples would be schools treating boys like pre-predators and Moms not teaching boys how to take care of themselves). Never heard the term?

I hadn't either. But WHY? Is it because we have a lot of trouble

seeing men as victims of anything?

 Tertullian - a father of the church describes women as "the gateway

of the devil" but also "a temple built over a sewer". You got to give

the guy points for creativity. Is it because female humans poop? I

know we are overly polite but our bodies do more then male bodies

do.

Rapist is a word but not Rapee. Would it correctly be raper and

Rapee? There is no label for the one it is done to, just the person

doing the action. My little brain is so confused. Please keep in mind,

if you keep reading, that I am doing the best I can with the brain I've

got.

At 49 years old, I look out on a landscape littered with the remains of

what men thought they would be. That's my dating pool, men

crushed by jobs, women and life. Every time I see a man driving a

nice car I wonder if he is supporting his children. Yep, I'm a little

jaded. I am trying to create something valuable for people with this

book.

A man can take a woman's life with a drop of sperm. I know, it happened to me. Am I an authority on men? Nah, I don't think so. To be that, I would have to be (a.) a man and (b.) have some formal education where some pompous ass says "Yup, you've got it". Caution...not educationally "man approved". I'm just a regular person that did a bunch of research and tried to make a point about something that is very important to me. I'm talking about the mysterious person that is man. Literally man, male, not the mankind man.

"If you never move, you never notice you are in chains" James Hattrick, more "So with our heads held aloft, noses to the sky, we acknowledge and disregard our miserable history for what it was. A time in our lives when we thought every girl we met was the one, and people only watched the television when they were stoned." The grifters.org

I long ago stopped believing that what I feel matters, I can only assume that many men feel this orders of magnitude more then I do. I still wonder why I consistently get sexually harassed, even where I work now. I just ignore it because I know they don't mean any harm but do I have to feel bad for not being interested in married men? If harassing single women is what married men do, why do I want one of my own?

More importantly, I am angry. I can't watch anymore while good people get sucked into bad systems that are no longer what the public wanted when they created them. The short list: Schools, jails, food suppliers and growers, and hospitals are heading that way. Major systems are broken and men let it happen. Take some responsibility - any woman can show you how.

Unfortunately the way my brain works is more like a puppy playing then like a train on tracks like it should be. Here goes a book anyway. Perhaps it will be funny because it's so bad.

Internet note: no, I am not going to kill myself, yes I'm probably a stupid whore, I am fat, I am too thin, I haven't seen my thigh-gap since middle school, I am a horrible parent for publishing a book while my daughter is twelve (why can't I wait?), I am getting male pattern baldness, I think I have my toenail fungus finally gone (thank God), I had hemorrhoids after childbirth, I still don't have my body back that I had before having a child, my facial hair is getting more robust every year, I'm lazy, I am horrible at conflict resolution, I was a Young Republican, I have smoked pot, I need to see my therapist more but my insurance no longer covers that (so when a patient dies at work I just have to get over it), I have a bunch of my paintings on a website that probably are no good, my passport is expired and I have a lot to learn.

I realized the other day, during a buzz-feed video, that men cannot go and hang out at a park alone where there are children playing. Protective Moms may attack them. That is completely true and completely wrong! I guess I am awakening late in life to the realization that men have these kinds of restrictions. Why can't they put on Chapstick in public? When did this start? No wonder nice dudes are hiding in their parent's basements. It turns out there are many things like this once you start looking. If I had known it would go this far, I probably wouldn't have started.

I want to shed light on these issues and ask the question "Is this really the way we all want things to be?" Do we really want to abandon all these minds, souls and possibly great dicks to video games, alcohol and drugs?" Is it because we have so limited men's options in the real world? At least Barbie got a house and stuff.

My style-hair Miss America doll dated the Six Million Dollar Man. He just took her places in her car. I had no idea what else he might do. What are men supposed to do? I have no idea but I'm hoping it involves cooking. I hate cooking.

I hope to make a case on why we need to change things and throw out possible solutions. One of my favorite books is the Quest for Cosmic Justice by Thomas Sowell here is a nice quote from it: "What the American Constitution established was not simply a particular system but a process for changing systems, practices and leaders, together with a method of constraining whoever or whatever was ascendant at any given time. Viewed positively, what the American Revolution did was to give the common man a voice, a veto, elbowroom, and a refuge from the rampaging presumptions of his 'betters'. That is why it was not simply a national phenomenon but has been seen by others in the world at large as a landmark in the general struggle for human freedom." This is one small example of why Thomas Sowell rocks! (I do need a dictionary as a reference to read some of his stuff though). As long as men and women keep squaring off from opposite corners of a boxing ring we ignore that

some of our basic rights are being trampled. There are

advertisements, magazines, TV shows and YouTube channels that

feed the idea that we need to protect us from the opposite sex. It's

big money. Let's take it away and make them sell us something

better.

Some basics that drive me, in no particular order: I am searching in

myself for a willingness, a wanting, to see a man of my age naked -

I'm pretty sure they feel the same way about me. Men have a long

history of being in charge. Males have not protected the females and

children overall. I know that some have, and kudos to you rare

animal! Something else needs to take it's place where both men and

women are respected like the people we are, not just a market

segment. People founded this great nation...those tough frontier men

would have died or died out, without women. Women still don't get

many props for that. We weren't just knitting while the men did all

the work (not that knitting is easy). Many men seem to need to

dominate women to feel like men. How sad that these men can't be

people in their own right. How sad that some men don't even want to change anything about our world to be people. That, in the absence of a war to fight or perimeter to protect, they lash out at the people being nice to them like spoiled little beasts (I'm talking to you Mr. Donovan- more on him later). We have abundant resources so we need a different model for society.

War seems inappropriate in times of plenty as does pointing fingers at others because our society has become something we don't like. I get that I may be naive and I have been told that it is not in men's nature to be caring and work in the industries that women are the guts of: healthcare, education and the workers of many industries. Can we stop there and just admit that they don't want to because it doesn't pay well for the grueling work that it is? While we are at it, let's stop telling girls that they are broken so we have to fix them (while ignoring boys or labeling them as a threat). Let's get some education going, this benefits both boys and girls in their glorious differences in the way they learn. Can we please stop pushing them both to be the same and let them be individuals with choices? It turns out that sexual orientation is not necessarily black and white - and has nothing to do with the shades of grey book and movie about domestic abuse. We are highly adaptable beings who are sadly more likely to act out of fear, then to go towards joy.

There is a great movement of feminism that is pushing equality for women and I consider myself a fan of that movement (or I just want to be paid more then men - screw equally!). I think it's silly to think that you can actually separate men's and women's rights. I am not interested in degrading men to give women better positions. There is enough room in this world for everybody. Speaking of everybody...

How did we completely lose track of the fact that someone has to raise children? If reproduction were just a woman's problem there would be no next generation. Do we need a shortage of children to force a better system? If you look at the statistics (cleaver little things that you can make say anything), I think we are getting it. Security and knowing that your children will probably survive (every country except the U.S. And Papa New Guinea even keep you out of poverty to raise kids) results in lower birth rates worldwide. I'm not an economist but a shortage of workers generally means they must be paid better.

After reading a book "The Way of Men" by Jack Donovan, I

understand better why men want to quickly define "us" and "them"

draw a perimeter and protect valuables like women and food. I have

never been treated as valuable by a male, so I figure I should just take

care of myself. I guess that makes me bad and evil in the eyes of

men. (I farted in front of a man I had been dating for two years by

accident on a camping trip and he was MAD. Wtf?) So if we can't

have continual war, Jack Donovan wants to take his toys and leave -

just take your hate for women you can't dominate and go and take

your fans with you. I think you dudes are underestimating

yourselves, women and what your lives can be if we can play nice

together.

Where I started in life, with my Dad...he displayed exactly two

emotions: anger and busy with something else (aka drinking). I spent

years wondering why I would want a man of my own if these are

their abilities? I was sheltered and even thought he kept rocks in his

underwear in case we were attacked in the middle of the night. What

else could be in there? Here are all the parenting talks I had (mom

was not helpful) from about age ten "Shut up", "Have a beer" and failing the first two, "Get the fuck out". It didn't get much better for me in the man department probably because I was a jerk, immature and didn't know how to act. I'm not sure I can actually believe that someone could love me. My daughter does and that completely blows my mind.

I have known many men...one lost one hundred pounds to date me, one hung himself a week after I broke up with him, a couple raped me (one in front of a group of his friends), a couple proposed marriage and wanted a pile of kids (I was told I couldn't have any), and some were crazy. My first boyfriend of five years doused himself in gasoline and walked into a campfire a few years ago. I wish I were making this stuff up. I am average looking so I don't get why married men hit on me? Am I the free entertainment? Do I look like I would help them cheat? (No way am I playing with anyone else's toys!) Men are sometimes fond of saying that all women are crazy...pot...kettle? I'm just saying be careful with your pointing dudes. I do get that the things that these men did in my life were not really about me. Perhaps not about me at all but I feel guilty just the same because somehow I let them happen.

I am taking the opportunity of having a child on my own to take a step back after refusing her fathers marriage proposal ("we can get married or whatever you want" after she was two months old and he had moved three states away) to examine exactly what I'm looking for in a man. What do I want in a relationship and exactly, what do I have to offer that a man would want? (Boobs, vagina?). Men should hold out for more then just parts It has quickly led me to ask, "What the heck is up with men?" Seriously, we have the most men in jail of any country in the world, of those that are loose, fewer and fewer of them have jobs. Many times more men commit suicide then women. Why? Many are violently unhappy and willing to harm others. Alarmingly few men are choosing to attend college (less then 30 percent). Are there no honorable men left? Is a better question "are there any honorable role models left?" When was the last time a leading man in a movie was a truly honorable man? Maybe I watch too much Comedy Central (not possible!). Is there any chance that we can figure out what would make life better for men and make it happen so that we can all be happier and save billions of dollars and lots of victims? I'm not going to go on and on about victims rights but I think we all know they don't really get any.

The way I have come to see things is that we offer men a tiny little cage of options they an be in life and wonder why they are not happy. Did anyone ever stop to consider why so many women of my generation got raped? Were we perhaps damaging boys and young men in some way? Can we figure this shit out rather then condemning half our population?

We judge men by how much money they have and women by what they look like. It would be hard to not do better if we just try a little bit.

Things are so much better for me now. I got out of college at a time when there were no jobs, started as a receptionist and worked my way up to account manager for a big account and promptly (ok three years) got burned out. The important lesson was that I was happier away from my family. But I still needed their love so bad. I spent a long time getting what I craved most - physical affection but I had no idea what to do with an actual caring person. It was totally foreign to me. It still totally fascinates me when I see a father spending time talking to his daughter. It just didn't happen in my experience. I would write my drunk Dad emotional-tear stained letters but got no response. So I felt worthless. I am no longer that hurt little girl (?).

Not one cell of my body is the same. They have all been made new

so why do the memories still have some power? I need to get all Elsa

on them and let them go!

I am actually very lucky in so many ways. I have a fully functional

body (I am assuming my lady bits still work, I have no privacy), mind

(probably) and I live in the United States where anything really is

possible. I get massages from a nice man named Ted that doesn't

know that he is helping to emotionally heal me with his wonderful

touch. I want to tell him but then we both might feel awkward.

I would like to say I am an artist. It seems like a title so big that

someone else should give it to you. I have been painting in acrylic on

canvas since 1984. I have a closet full of paintings that I don't show

people. I have given a couple away as gifts but I have never sold a

painting. I can't let them go. I don't know why. I do not hoard

anything else at this time (ok some Lego mini figures) but, I have a

little house so I should probably at least try to sell paintings. I sold

all my jewelry and stocks to pay for health insurance when I was pregnant. I guess I should try to let my paintings go too. They are at www.marcystudio.com if you are bored. It never occurred to me to apply for government money. I wanted to live in a way that my child would be proud of how I took care of her.

I had a daughter with a guy I dated for about a month. That month was December, so we met each other's families but he moved to Minnesota when I was five months pregnant. Yes, he knew I was pregnant and there was no question as to whose she was. He said via email "see you in nine months for a paternity test" changed his phone number and moved two states away. Yes my daughter is his according to the paternity test. At the time I got pregnant I was 35 years old, living in an ok apartment had my own business going making stained glass lamps and worked leasing apartments. I had just quit a consulting job that required tons of travel. I couldn't go back to traveling around (being pregnant then a Mom) but I loved that job. So I moved out of my apartment and into a storage until, quit my leasing job, turned down lamp work because the chemicals are bad for the baby, my lease was up on my car so I gave that up and moved in with my parents. My Dad was busy dying of colon cancer so I would sneak around to do his chores like mowing the lawn because he would feel bad if he saw me doing his jobs. I was so busy that I don't remember most of it. I know at some point a mowed the grass holding my baby because she wouldn't go to anyone else.

That's an awesome visual right? No house, no car, and no job and pregnant...then her dad moved two states away and did his best to forget that I exist. I think he's glad now that he has a daughter but I'm sure he'd be happier if I didn't exist. Ditto babe. The thing that is really weird is that his secret girlfriend in Minnesota made giant scrapbooks of my daughter's first two years of life. The man didn't even meet Maya until she was like two months old and didn't pay the first year because he didn't want to "pay the wrong amount". He sued me for full custody because I used profanity when she was a baby. (To him when I said "Fuck no" when he sort of proposed) I thought - really is that all you got? I was also hauled into court and had to answer to a bunch of men why was I still breastfeeding when she was almost a year old? My goal, despite working full time, was to nurse for at least a year because her dad is allergic to everything. He said I was doing it just so that he couldn't have an overnight visit with the baby that clearly hated his guts (but she would go to everyone else - babies know).

I sold out of all my retirement and jewelry paying for Cobra health insurance and finally found a job when I was seven months pregnant. Have you ever been shopping for maternity-interview clothes? I have. Have you ever had to pump breast milk in a bathroom stall three times a day? Oh, I got the job thank God! My insurance started the first of the month and she was born the 26th. I went back to work one week after my C-section because I had no leave and I wanted to keep my job. Thank God for the super-nice people at that job!

I busted my bottom working, helping with my Dad, working and went to full-time school for two years (working full-time for free at my clinical and working part-time) to become a Radiographer. My Dad died during my honors ceremony. My Mom tried to get me to still go to the stupid thing - I was top of my class. That just shows you how you really can't think clearly dealing with someone dying like that. I didn't walk at graduation the next day either. I just couldn't do anything without crying for a bit. I still miss my Dad. He hated my daughter's Dad with a passion I have only seen him display when watching Fox News. I sometimes wonder what my dad would have done to her dad if he had had the strength before he died. Would my daughter have received something because her dad was in the army?

Can someone please come up with some quick and easy hacks for men to make their lives easier so they quit being such childish jerks? Someone who has actually lived longer then a mere forty years please. I am curious how much I will be hated and for what when I publish this. Maybe I will get one of those cool games where people can virtually beat me to a pulp. Is there a rape one yet?

If men hadn't been such dicks about dominating women from the start, we wouldn't need feminism now. What about just people equality? Stop pitting us against each other. Schoolboys are sometimes labeled as pre-batterers and horrible things, simply because they are boys. What came first, you calling them villains of their bad behavior? Is "peopleism" a thing? My spell check says no.

According to Bloomberg Business article "The economic Power of Positive Thinking by Charles Kenny, Looking beyond income, there's been enough progress over the last generation to be optimistic about the next one. The violent crime rate is a quarter the level it was in the early 1990s. Over the past three decades, life expectancy, in rich countries around the world has climbed by six years."

I know that I have "broken some hearts" in my life. I'm sure most people have. I just want to say that none of it was premeditated or on purpose. I am fundamentally bad at relationships, understanding when someone likes me and I have really a lot to learn. I pray that someday I get another chance to get to know a nice man.

Finally, a quote by Helen Smith in her book Men on Strike "A boy today, through no fault of his own, finds himself implicated in the social crime of 'shortchanging' girls. Yet the allegedly silenced and neglected girl sitting next to him is likely to be a better student. She is not only more articulate; she is probably a more mature, engaged, and well-balanced human being. He may be uneasily aware that girls are more likely to go to college. He may believe that teachers prefer to be around girls and pay more attention to them. At the same time, he in uncomfortable aware that he is considered to be a member of the unfairly favored 'dominant gender'."

2 GET IN THE PIT AND TRY AND LOVE SOMEONE!

We judge men by how well they handle the little box we give them, they take on hobbies like golf, cycling, sports watching and gaming. Who wins? Follow the money. If men chose to be more engaged in meaningful relationships more often, how would that impact our society? How many men want more out of life then dying alone with a controller in their hand? I think the general unrest has found a community online called the "Manosphere". It's gaining popularity every day. I would love to see men get more out of their lives. I know that the manosphere gets a bad reputation as being tips for pick up artists but I found it to be much more then that.

Girls grow up learning about all the great men of history and all that they have accomplished through the rose colored glasses of time that tends to leave behind their less appetizing qualities. Women are seldom mentioned except as in relation to the great men. So women are nothing and men do everything? Then we try to date these amazing historical creatures and they don't even talk, let alone inspire respect. I feel cheated when they say, "we are simple" and "boys will be boys" really? So all the good dudes are dead? The guys that made all of the history that woman don't seem to have been part of? WTF. Probably the history book writers took their wives for granted that we're keeping them and their children fed while the man wrote history stuff.

You can't have it both ways...either men or simple or they are great. Which ONE would you like?

Men have it worse then women do (though not financially). Since virtually all characters in sit coms, video games and movies exist only in relation to the men in the stories with no character or thought of their own. Then they get ahold of an actual woman and they are people with thoughts and feelings and nowhere near the prefect photo-shopped bodies they have been told are their due by virtue of having a penis. It must be horrible. I can see why they would be mad that we are 1,000 times more complicated then they thought, don't wake up looking like supermodels and have bodies that look like a deflated balloon once we have kids. You have to admit that women are pretty generous in the looks department with what they will accept from men and perhaps more importantly, so is society. What would happen if both our looks were equally important? Could we all just be people? I know advertising consistently reminds us that if we have cellulite or thinning hair that we should just buy their stuff or curl up and die.

Men see things fundamentally differently then I do. Where I see a people problem, they generally see a thing problem, resource problem or structural problem. I think where women tend to see and manage people, men tend to see things and resources. My general thought is that the strongest enterprise is one that plays to both of those equally important strengths. Because of technology, the last two decades have been especially turbulent in the work areas that men are good at. I would assume that they are still reeling and trying to find a happy place in all that mess. So are women. Our only hope is to work together...for divided we fall.

Places where women provide most of the workers that have been protected so far are being thrust into all the turbulence - healthcare, education and shift workers of many kinds. Our pay is already lower. If you have clothes on you can probably thank a women or a child. I think the world is moving towards having to compensate more workers fairly. This should get interesting.

The world will eventually run our of workers willing to kill themselves for low pay and accepting part-time so the employer doesn't have to provide benefits (I'm looking at you Wal-Mart and many hospitals).

Men also have a beautiful stoicism that is empowering and useful for life. When faced with something that doesn't give them some reward they want (money, sex, space, power) they will avoid it for as long as possible, then do it badly. The response is "I'm never asking that guy to do that again!" Mission accomplished. It's brilliant! The first time it sucks but then for the rest of time - it's covered! I would really rather they just say why they don't want to do it. I have unrealistic expectations, I get it. I'd really like men to re-visit parenting. Why do all parents get separated from our children so that they can learn what the state wants them to know? Can there be more opportunities to apprentice with a parent? Talk about new ways of looking at things in a fast changing world! Rant done, back to what I like about men.

Forbes.com "stoic week organizer Donald Robertson says nudged many curious readers towards stoicism. Robertson, a Scottish-born therapist and classics enthusiast, led workshops on psychological resilience for managers at oil giant Shell called "How to Talk Like a Roman Emperor." Based on the life of stoic philosopher-king Marcus Aurelius' life embodied these five stoic ideals. 1. Immediately recognize what is out of your control. 2. Fear, anger and other emotions are personal choices, regardless of outer circumstances. 3. Live a life centered on principles, not wealth, awards, family or power. 4. People who misbehave do not deserve an emotional reaction from you. 5. Meditate daily to revive your commitment to a people-centered life.

Stoicism is actually vital for a happy life. It is that thing that lets you move on from the sucky things that happen to all of us. There is such a tragedy in being stuck in life. You just keep giving more power to whatever the sucky thing was. The tragedy is that you miss so much that is good and enjoyable while you are stuck on one bad thing, no matter how valid that thing is. Synonyms: patience, forbearance, resignation, fortitude, endurance, acceptance, tolerance - take your pick. I just read about a study done in the late 1990s that said that stoicism is actually linked with better emotional health! Yay! Huge sign of relief! Is this what is missing from our children's upbringing.... the ability to get over it and move on? Are they literally singing "Let it Go"...from Disney? Yes, let's try that for a change rather then all of this self absorbed blubbering! Apparently if you force yourself to move on, it's actually good for you!

Aeon.co/magazine Indifference is a power: "As legions of warriors and prisoners can attest, stoicism is not grim resolve but a way to wrest happiness from adversity." Larry Wallace: "the truth is, indifference really is a power, selectively applied, and living in such a way that is not only eminently possible, with a conscious adoption of certain attitudes, but facilitates a freer, more expansive, more adventurous mode of living. Joy and grief are still there, along with all the other emotions, but they are tempered - and, in their temperance, they are less tyrannical." 99u.com 1/26/2015. "The stoics focus on two things: 1. How can we lead a fulfilling, happy life? And, 2. How can we become better human beings? Acknowledge that all emotions come from within, find someone you respect and use him or her to stay honest, recognize that there is life after failure (no failure, no growth). Read purposefully and apply your knowledge, challenge yourself to be brutally honest. Reflect on what you spend the most time on, remind yourself to be brutally honest, reflect on what you spend the most time on, remind yourself: you weren't meant to procrastinate, put the phone away and be present, time is your most precious resource."

We women feel bad about doing anything badly, like ever. Love is being perfect to many women. Nope, that's not love. I would never ask that of someone, why do we think we need to provide this? Before we women agree to trade our every waking minute for things that don't benefit us in any way we need to think a bit more about our own sanity. Nobody likes a martyr. No wonder the world isn't a better place yet; we are all doing stupid stuff that doesn't align with our priorities. We owe it to our selves to live them. I have learned so much about love from my daughter. I would never ask her to be perfect or not make mistakes. She would never expect those things from me. I about turned myself inside out trying to be perfect so that I would get some love growing up. I assumed there was love there to get. That's a really hard lesson. I was my parents second failed attempt at having a boy child.

I love the fact that most men are physically stronger then me. It is unfortunate in some ways that this ability is rarely needed for most jobs. The jobs that do require body strength don't serve men for long because their backs or other body parts can't tolerate the abuse for long. I am a single mom and I have access to YouTube so yes I can learn how to do stuff. All the stupid tools are built for hands bigger then mine. For example "step 1 snap piece A into piece B" um sure with who's hands? The battery packs on most hand tools are too fragging heavy to hold up for any length of time. I have to wax poetic about one drill made by the Skill corporation that was perfect - it had a light, it was light, it was powerful ahhh alas they don't make it anymore. Used ones are $90.00 on eBay without a charger. We had our chance I guess. My drill after only seven years of projects will only go in reverse. It's so sad really.

Men know how to get paid to stand around a hole by the side of the road doing nothing. I have never seen a job posting for this. I have never seen a women standing around a hole doing nothing. Why do six men need to stand around a hole watching, usually the smallest guy there, dig the hole? What the hay is in there besides a little guy digging? Is the secret to how to do math in there? Naked coeds? Juggling monkeys? I don't get it but I admire that they figured out how to get paid very well for it. They are better compensated then daycare workers and home-care staff. I bet if we put kids and the elderly in the hole the men would run away. But the kids would be easier to find...hmmm.

Caution...bitch rant...you may want to skip...I may be spending too much time in my car but here is another one...they endlessly park vehicles in the roadway because it's more convenient for them then parking. I get that the trees need to be trimmed, trash needs to be picked up, deliveries need to be made etc. but with a little communication you could park in a driveway instead of holding up traffic. The people taking care of your kids have places to be. It can only be their effortless recto-cranial inversions that I admire. Roads are for driving, period.

Men learn a million things growing up that girls don't: Mainly about cars but also lawn mowers and home maintenance and repair. Then there is the assumed knowledge that is probably more valuable then their actual knowledge...a mechanic will assume that they know something about fixing cars and a home repair person will assume the same and give them an actual fair price on repair jobs. Chicks end up paying Angie's list or getting taken. I don't want to God forbid get all feminist but could we have a class in high school that covers some of these basics that we all need to know? Can we leave school more functional? Not just older? That is another book though.

I admire that men learned not to cry and, more then that, many are able to completely ignore crying in others and act like that is the kindest way to handle the situation. At least offer me a tissue, you douche doctor. I'm probably just bitter because when I get mad, I cry. Why can't I just be mad? Even when I have a good reason to be mad, I cry. It is so frustrating. I guess I'm afraid of my own emotion? Then I have to be alone for a minute, and then I can finally say what made me mad. Why can't I just say it to start with? I guess it's ok that a hug makes everything better with me 99% of the time. I am working on learning to be more stoic if you couldn't tell.

Men automatically command attention, respect and are seen as more intelligent just because they are taller (in general). I bet short men will agree with me on this one (I'm sorry that no amount of working out will make you taller). How is it that the ability to reach stuff that's up high means so much in our society? It's crazy. Was there THAT much food up in trees that we needed these tall dudes to get it down for us? At my age now, I'm not sure I want to have to wash all that extra fabric to do the wash of a tall man. Ok, either short or self-sufficient just got added to my list of qualities I would like in a mate.

Men seem to be pathologically unable to tell you what you want to hear. Politicians being the exception here - they should use their powers for good but often don't. They also don't get so invested in other people's problems that they forget their own priorities. I need a tattoo that says "Not my circus, not my monkeys" and I don't even have very many friends. I think it's fair to say that in general people like to try to fix other people's problems but, in general, men are less likely to get sucked down someone else's rabbit hole. Example: Some random dude named Ed "Dude, my wife just died" other random guy after an uncomfortable silence "That sucks, wanna play golf?" Sure. That's the end of it. It must save them so much time! I hope they are all not wasting all of their extra time worrying about loosing their hair. I have talked to very few women that care about men's hair. Looks like less work to me. Why don't you go to the library and learn something so you are more interesting?"

Men are fearless when it comes to playing video games. Naturally! I am such a sissy worrying that I will do something wrong It's just a stupid game but it brings out my robust and well-developed worrying about looking stupid beast, that stops me from doing and trying stuff. I guess their fearlessness in general I admire. I don't know what age they start practicing a poker face but they are generally way ahead of me. I don't even have any sort of decent filter between my brain and my mouth.

Men's clothes are less trend-dependent, better made and they always get pockets. I love pockets! I buy men's lounge pants and sew up the fly to have pockets in my lounging pants. They put fake pockets in women's clothes! Is this a terrorist plot? What idiot decided that was ok? This needs to stop! We are real actual people and we need the same from our pockets. Oops tangent. Anyway, why the general quality differences? Women pay more - their clothes should last longer and have real pockets! Clothing equality now please! I won't even rant about standardizing sizing.

There are clear social expectations most of the time for men's clothes. Chicks just don't get that. There is a great video by Jenna Marbles where she does a rap song that she's got three looks: hooker, young boy or homeless person...it's hilarious and worth your time. Caution, YouTube is highly addictive.

Their dressy clothes don't make you wonder if they are selling sexual favors. They may look like the waiter sometimes but their shoes don't hobble them in less then an hour. Dinner and dancing? ...Ok if

the walk from the car isn't too far. I have herd at some trendy clubs

in New York that closing time looks like a bunch of zombies from a

Michael Jackson video with girls carrying their shoes and moaning.

This is when you guys are trying to get us to go home and have sex

with you. All we can think about is our aching feet. The pain doesn't

stop the minute you take the shoes off. The shoes look awesome but

ouch! Who feels like sexy time when then want their feet amputated

so they will hurt less? Can we have some change to this situation so

that everyone gets lucky more often? I've seen one place in my life

that is dinner and dancing for grown ups. Can that happen more?

They wear the same clothes and shoes for years. I can't imagine how

much money this saves! Their clothes are so much better in quality

that they actually LAST for years! Given that we get 78% of the pay

of men, you would think it would be women that were wearing the

same clothes for years! I work in healthcare so luckily I get to wear

scrubs. We could offer office workers some sort of option like

scrubs? Just because you don't get puked, bled or pooped on at

work, doesn't mean a standard outfit wouldn't make things easier. I think men kind of already do that with a button-down and kakis. I

really don't want anyone to tell me what I have to wear so I guess

there is that.

Men's self-maintenance costs are lower in terms of time and money,

Dramatically lower. We should learn from dudes and learn to keep it

simple but we all know the bar for looks is set a bit higher for us

chicks. It's the reverse of the golf tee situation. I have no interest in

bringing men up to where we are, that would be silly. I think

younger men may be moving in that direction. I hope that I am

wrong. I would be lying if I didn't state right here that man-scaping

scares me. I get that men can make fun designs on their faces -

maybe chicks should do the same with their leg hair...hmmmm. Oh

wait the point was men please leave your junk alone! Feel free to

keep the back hair under control - um we need to grab you there

sometimes...

It would be funny if it were a normal thing that, when you are invited

to an event, you are told exactly what to wear right down to the

brand and model number. Your only choice is size. You would

really be at the mercy of your host! For example: a football party where everyone was required to wear black Hanes sweats - crew neck top, elastic waist pants. What would that be like? We can call them OP's (outfit parties obviously). Would that do anything to lower people's social anxiety? Feels a little conformist and socialist but if these people are part of your personal tribe, would that make it ok? I keep hearing lately that everyone has social anxiety like 90% of people to some extent. Are there more options for solutions then alcohol and drugs? Come on, we are all smart creative people here! Can we have video gamers and fashion designers do some job trading? It could be sweet for both!

Men have always had the strength to go to war. I admire men that are willing to put their life on the line for what they believe. It is unconscionable and horrible that Veterans are not treated better here in the US. I wonder if we are paying more for our prisoners or our vets. I tried to find the info but I failed. Are we forcing some veterans into criminal behavior because we don't take care of them? Could someone smarter then me please figure this out? I heard a story on the radio this morning of a soldier that was forced to walk for miles in a frozen environment by his leader and he lost three of his toes. He now gets $40K per year until he dies. How do they pick that amount? I'm ok with him getting the money, it probably hurt a lot and he could have gotten an infection all over his body from that wound (sepsis) or died. I also think that by learning to work together we can make war less necessary. If we had a government that was actually FOR the people instead of USING the people we would take better care of our veterans. It makes me really mad that we don't treat these men and women with the respect and reverence that they deserve. I could go on and on but I won't.

Many men have the general bravery that they can hunt and kill things. I don't understand how they do it. I can't kill anything that crunches in a squishy way.

In my head hunting is always done as the Indians did it. With great honor and respect. I try my best to ignore stories of beer drenched accidental shootings. I try to not assume things about all men from these stories.

I once read a great story of the right of passage of a young American Indian male. I'm sure I won't do it justice but in the story he fasted for two days and then began to track a deer over the course of days. Eating nothing, and I believe he took some kind of mushroom before beginning. He noticed every habit and movement of the deer. Focusing only on the deer until they became one. Until the warrior could be mere feet from the deer without it minding. Until he knew what the deer would do at every turn. Only then when, when he was one with the animal, did he respectfully and quickly without a fight, take the animal's life. I feel it's such a momentous and powerful story of the young American Indian becoming a man. What do we now offer our young men and women? Repressed sex information or abstinence-based education and a more detailed dress code (well, for girls at least).

I put men who know how to fish in a completely different category. Is it fair to say that they are quite a different type of man? I see them as patient and kind, willing to spend an afternoon or morning quietly waiting for a bite. Something about learning to be still. Makes me think they might be good listeners. I totally don't and probably never will understand sport fishing. It just seems like showing off and wasting huge resources (they may, for all I know, fund the protection of more wetlands then anyone else, actually that would be cool). I know how to clean fish well but catching them seems to get away from me (rim shot please). I have trouble sitting for that long.

Possibly the main thing that I love about men is that most of them usually want sex. I didn't fully appreciate how great this is until I was in my thirties. I actually think chicks think about it just as often as men but woman get a mental whammy growing up that says that is both wrong and bad. Only bad women want sex. So we distract ourselves with crafts and kids. How can I be horny when the wash isn't done? So of course, at least when I was growing up, sets up a battle of two opposing forces meaning people miss out on a whole lot of pleasure in this world. I think this is improving through the tireless work of people like Laci Green who has an awesome YouTube channel all about sex education that is completely devoid of judgments (or as close as a person can get). Am I thrilled that my twelve-year-old daughter knows tons more then I did? Yes actually. We were watching Pewdiepie (another YouTuber) the other day and

I said to my 12-year-old daughter "Jeez do all the women in The Forest game have to be topless? Why?" She said, "Because they don't discriminate". She's awesome. Canada is ahead of the US on allowing anyone to go topless.

Men are the main reason our species goes on. I'm not kidding. Most chicks' over-think things, especially when we are younger and if we had to do all of the asking we would be doomed as a species. I know that current young people are not as caught up in sexual stereotypes as people of my generation but they haven't been around long enough to see how they will change the world. For now we got to give props to dudes. At least they ask! They take on all the social anxiety and fear and ask! There are entire world for men online to learn tricks to get laid. Thank God I am "over the wall" meaning past the age where anyone is trying to pick me up.

When men are getting a new job, the expected response from men is negotiate for their salary and the expected response from women is to just take what is offered or not. Women are seldom taught to negotiate on their own behalf in America. If you can teach me how please do! I am writing this book as a way to get time with my daughter instead of a job. The message that I got growing up was that it is bad and rude to question what is offered to me – just take it or leave it. The mantra from adults around me when I was growing up: Shut up or get the fuck out.

Men are able to enjoy the Jackass movies. I have tried but I just wound up with a crush on Johnny Knoxville. I am completely serious and will watch them anytime but I'm just thinking about making out with him. I don't get why I can't get the humor. It is probably something drummed out of little girls of my age. Women are people too. Here's a deal, we will let you be people and you do the same for us. I know we haven't always been considered people and raping us has seldom been seen as a crime but we've gotten a taste of being people now and we like it! There is no going back! That does not mean that damaging men is necessary! There is not just one cake – it's a big world. Stronger women and men means stronger children and a stronger economy.

Men seem to naturally have a bigger appetite for risk. This is admirable and needed to balance out most women's strong tendency to focus on safety and security. This has been proven many times in investment clubs where equally weighted male/female clubs perform the best. Better then men only clubs or women only clubs. I think it's worth noting that we are stronger working together then either of us are apart.

Some men are able to love cars more then people. It's kind of special when they are preserving a valuable piece of history that they really enjoy; it's another when you choose the car over your wife and children. That is a special brand of crazy. I get that it is socially acceptable but it seems really passive-aggressive to me. I know lots of women hop on board and support their men on this and that's great. I am assuming their husbands are the dudes I see patiently waiting at craft shows and shopping malls. Often while holding a purse. I love those guys because they are clearly part of a team. Main point is it's none of my business how someone else orchestrates their happiness, I just hope there is some balance.

Men get to go shirtless a lot. This includes men of all shapes, sizes, and amounts of hairiness. I got to go topless once in Canadian waters (before I breast fed my daughter). It felt so great! I was on a boat at WaterPalooza where boats form a U-shape in Canadian waters and they put a floating stage at the top of the U with bands playing on it. It was so sweet! People on Jet skis were zipping across the middle visiting and in the morning the bigger boats with kitchens started passing around plates of bacon and eggs. I only went topless after it was dark and most people were asleep. It was long ago now, but it felt really great! I guess there is a downside to going topless - having to show your belly. Oh and I forgot all about moobs. Do men have anxiety about their bodies like women do? One would never know from how they act. We women should learn from them and just have a good time anyway. I have never seen a man shamed for wearing a bathing suit at the beach no matter how fat and hairy he is. Women should be able to be fat and hairy too.

3 O.F.F.S.R? (OH FOR FUCKS SAKE REALLY?)

"In line with the policy, British Airlines cabin crew patrols the aisles before takeoff checking that youngsters traveling on their own or in a different row from their parents are not next to a male stranger. If they find a man next to a child or teenager they will ask him to move to a different seat. The aircraft will not take off unless he obeys... Mr. Fischer, who lives in Luxembourg with his wife and their daughter Sophia said: 'This policy is branding all men as perverts for no reason. The policy and the treatment of male passengers is absolutely outrageous.'"

There are some shocking things going on with boys and men. Less then 30% are going to college, many are "going Gault" (I had to look this up so I read Atlas Shrugged by Ayn Rand. An absolutely awesome book!), many are staying in their parent's basements because they have experienced something that made them give up and say, "Fuck it". A job, a woman or bullies from school have left them feeling that they need to protect what little they feel they have left to offer the world that shuns them for being male, for being unnecessary for parenting and being a cog in someone else's wheel. No wonder they want to go save virtual topless damsels and shoot zombies. What the hell do we expect? What did males do with their time before video games?

Why do men so often resort to silence? We tell kids not to hit or bite but do we teach them how to express difficult or strong feelings? Psychology Today Five Reasons Men Go Silent by Shawn T. Smith PhD on May 31, 2013 "Men aren't supposed to talk, they feel outmatched, angry...It pains us to argue with you. I don't think many women realize just how important you are to us men (the good men anyway). An unhappy woman is a painful experience for many men. When the same old arguments show up repeatedly, we start to feel powerless about keeping you happy. That's when some men go silent. Also, holding on to masculinity." I assume this is part of what you agree to for a "Man Card". Is this concept really serving men?

Did you guy really give up on talking about things you care about so easily? What did you get for it? Beer?

Where do men start to get the idea that women have them outmatched when it comes to talking? Is this a reality or an unearned perception? Females get a lot more practice putting our feelings into words then men do. Indeed we are "allowed" to use any words we want. Seems like men are restricted on what they are allowed to feel, let alone express.

Well, that makes me not want to get married! I get that I am childish and lazy. I don't have time to chase around silent Bob wondering what he's thinking while trying not to feel abandoned. Can you please learn to talk? Repeat after me "I need some time to think, can we talk at 5:00?" You can't just request an indefinite amount of time to stall but everyone needs a break to think before talking about things that are really important to them. If you just let things marinate and don't talk about them they fester and pollute your world. What's bugging you doesn't go away. It's about integrity to me. When you stop talking for long periods we women tend to assume things like you are plotting your permanent escape from the relationship, amassing a weapons cache, or thinking about having sex with the neighbors. Just remember that we chicks have imaginations too.

Women are accessories, non-playable characters and damsels in distress in most currant social narratives. Don't men want more out of a partner then that? Of course we want to know where we stand with you - main character that you are. We know that talking makes us feel better so we are trying to make you feel better by getting you to talk but if you just need to think, you will probably need to tell us that. I don't have my head all the way up my ass, I can see that the last thing you want to do when you are angry/depressed is reassure your woman that things are ok. We have invested our most valuable resource in you - time.

"United States, 2013 research. Depression receives significantly less in research funds from the US National Institutes of Health then do cancer or heart disease. That is partly because of a lack of patient advocates and the stigma that surrounds the condition." I get it. In my last work review I was told that I am "not happy enough at work." I am a single mom that never gets a day with her child unless my daughter stays home "sick" from school. I have worked almost every weekend of the last four years and I am burned out. I have not been laid this year. Dudes generally want to have sex. Can we figure out some man-share program for single moms that can't get out? Can we have an app and call it Uber/Under? Ha! I get it; it's sort of prostitution, what if we just barter? I've been reading lately that depression is all about a problem with the bugs that live in our guts? I'm serious. What if antibiotic consumption (in our food) and use is heavily linked with the suicide rate? Is it the highest in red meat eaters eating cows that are fed only corn when they are supposed to eat only grass? Chickens are supposed to eat bugs not just corn and chemicals. It was probably all ok until the corn got classified as a insecticide. How about we get our food back on track and see what changes?

I need to ask the question "is our ignoring mental health hurting more men or more women?" You could successfully argue either but we need programs that work for both. Again, you can't just fix part of a problem and expect smooth sailing.

Nature.com News 11/24/2014. "Mental Health: A world of

depression - 'A global view of the burden caused by depression' by

Kerri Smith 12 November 2014. Depression is a major human

blight. Globally, it is responsible for more 'years lost' to disability

then any other condition. This is largely because so many people

suffer from it - some 350 million, according to the World Health

Organization - and the fact that it lasts for many years. (When

ranked by disability and death combined, depression comes in ninth

behind prolific killers such as heart disease, stroke, and HIV). Yet

depression is widely undiagnosed and untreated because of stigma,

lack of effective therapies and inadequate mental health resources.

Almost half the worlds population lives in a country with only two

psychiatrists per 100,000 people." Depression is a real thing that

devastates lives and strains our economy. Can we please treat it as

such? It needs to be ok for anyone to seek treatment. Only after you

have tried every treatment possible, should you apply for disability.

Because being on disability is really bad for you and sets a horrible

example for your children. I motivate myself all the time by asking

myself what I would want my daughter to do. It's easier to see a clear

path without myself in the way. I don't want to squander the

blessing that is being born in the United States.

I have been reading extensively on our microbiome and it may be that women suffer more depression because we are too disconnected from the dirt. I know it sounds nuts. This is just my theory as far as I know but our soil, our dirt acts as our external digestive system. We are in no way alone. Our gut and bodily bugs outnumber our human cells 10 to 1. Some people with horrible diseases can be cured with a hookworm infestation. We have a lot to learn and many reasons for hope right now. Don't despair right before the solution.

Back to men – they have Autism approximately five times as often as females (that is one in sixty eight boys these days!) It is just so fascinating that our gut and bodily bugs do so much to make us who we are and we don't have a clue which ones are good, bad, required or accessories. Probably depends what DNA you have to know what bugs you need to feel good. Gut microbiome organisms. Have already been strongly linked to depression. If I make any money from this book, I am going to go study that! So excited! What if I can help figure out what our internal micro-gardens are supposed to look like?

Here, in America, the NIH (National Institute of Health) could do it this way: give funding to research to diseases in terms of how many U.S. Citizens are affected (using the put your own air mask on first so that you can help others thought process). It is not political nor is it that fucking hard. If a research body doesn't perform for two years in a row then they go to the bottom of the pile and give someone else a chance. Can something be done with our money benefit **us** for once? I think those "working" in government have enough of everything. The study of our body bugs affects many of our organ systems and could be the key to many diseases. This study has benefitted greatly from the human genome projects (that's the only way we have to figure out what bugs are living in our guts). I'm sorry I went off on a big tangent. Let's get back to dudes.

Men are much less likely to say, "I don't know". Why? They don't want to appear weak? Why is it considered weak not to know something? That's not weak. What's weak is believing your own bullshit. They are also less likely to help another person out. (It's not an accusation I found a study so it must be true). What kind of messed up thing is that? Or is it something we need to learn? I don't think it's a bad thing to hold people accountable if you help them. Just refusing to help someone is really hard for me. Perhaps a fundamental difference between men and women. This is another reason why we need each other – to fairly evaluate situations and allocate resources.

World population is approximately seven billion people according to the world population clock on November 26, 2014. CIA World fact book, total male estimate as of July 2013 is 3,571,374,099 ratio is 1.01 males to every female. The numbers say we should find ways to make society work better for males.

US Census 2010 most recent "since census 2000, the population has continued to grow older, with many states reaching a median age over 40 years. At the same time, increases in the number of men are apparent." I've been reading so much about men but haven't learned much that is useful to me. Most recently, "7 Things Your Man Won't Ever Tell You." It's all about how men want respect, to be needed and appreciated. But this man thinks women want affection (as different from sex), love, and to talk and be heard. What if I am a woman that wants exactly what men want? Can I get that please? He actually says that men are just boys inside so you have to treat them very carefully. Why do men not have to grow up? I don't want to grow up either! Why is this automatically added to the woman's responsibilities? What if we have our own issues like people do? Put them away in favor of everyone else's needs? Not healthy! It seems like a loving relationship should enable both people to have a safe place to land. Am I holding out for too much?

The Way of Men by Jack Donovan. "It has always been the job of men to draw the perimeter, to establish a safe space, to separate us from them and create a circle of trust." "In a complex society, almost all of us live deep within the perimeter. We create our own circles or cliques, and we defend them metaphorically." "When men evaluate each other as men, they still look for the same virtues that they'd need to keep the perimeter. Men respond to and admire the qualities that would make men useful and dependable in an emergency. Men have always had a role apart, and they still judge one another according to the demands of that role as guardian in a gang struggling for survival against encroaching doom. As you stand back to back, fending off incoming oblivion, what do you need from the men in your group? As you close a circle tighter around dangerous game that could feed you all for a week, what kind of men do you want at your flank?" What do these kind of men want from females? Oh yeah, they want women to take care of absolutely everything so that they can look for danger. Except that the danger is more subtle and cyber now – do our protectors take the time to learn what they can do against real threats to society? Do women? It's entirely possible, probable even, that I am a complete asshole and we really need near constant vigilance of our stadiums and golf courses.

Is this what men and video games are about? Dumb question probably. Let's look up some data most popular multiplayer game is....Dota 2 (Defense of the Ancients, counter-strike: Global Offensive, Team Fortress 2. Another place on Seam it says Call of Duty Advanced Warfare.

On Gizmopod here are the rankings: Eve 2, Guild Wars 2, Dark Fall: Unholy Wars, uk.askmen.com. "World of Warcraft is for plump cellar-dwellers, their pallid flab ribbed with grime; Minecraft for pimply miscreants who subsist on a diet of their own hangnails. They won't do. The following are video games for the multiplayer-hungry man; games that go boom, games awash in blood of thine real-life enemies (but often mostly your own, because you are frequently drunk and thus awful at aiming down the iron sight), games that stoke the fires of our most basic and enjoyable instinct as blokes." Ha-ha wow!

Are men ever mean to each other! If a woman said that to a man he would be traumatized for life. Can we come up with an application that teaches men how to talk about things that are important to them? Like a translator? You could blow up their character if they say the wrong thing. Women need man translators too. I would download that app.

What I conclude from the games that men play is that they want to be brave, heroic heroes and be tested. I think that is very hot! I see no place in current society other then video games where they can get this kind of feeling. I know some men find it in being Dads, politics, hunting or racing something. We need them to dive in and conquer our jacked up education and healthcare systems! Can we just admit that mostly chicks screwed them up with their tendencies to martyr themselves? Buying your own school supplies? Are you on crack?

Doing nothing but teaching to the next test? Arming children with

no skills for life? Let's call it a fail and move on! How the hell did

we get from kids having the summers off to work in the fields

(helping with the family survival) to a bus visiting a corner in my

neighborhood eight time per day and very strict drop off and pick up

times so that when both parents work, grandparents are mostly doing

it these days! Education is crippling families instead of helping them

succeed. Let's assume most of the parents have to work and design a

system from there. "The School System" needs to understand that

the first priority has to be the well being of the family – not the bus

schedule. The way we live now…all hail the mighty bus schedule!

Now I've pissed off enough people, let's talk about Manscaping. Let

it hide in the bushes where it is protected. It will come out when it's

ready. No one wants to see that soft thing anyway. Now show me a

beautiful, stunning panty-wetting hard one any day hell yes! But

soft...meh. It looks like I need to help you get it ready to play. Oh

good something else to do.

Please parents, stop cutting your little boys penis! Why would you want to take pleasure away from your own child? It should be a crime. Sex is one of the coolest things our bodies can do.

I doubt I am the only female who feels this way about manscaping. Many women don't have room for the extra length you think you get. All the talk about everyone having "hard wood floors" is ridiculous and unhealthy. I heard recently that the bush is coming back. God help me if I really need to worry if my privates are in style! Don't I just need to worry about works best for my partner and me? I am completely open to options: his name, colors not found in nature, etc. but if itches like I have a disease or infestation then I will take a pass. Which is what happens after you wax (a euphemism for torture).

Now beer-bellies are the speed bumps of love to me but little fat is preferable to a skinning guy for me. I have no interest in banging our hipbones together - ugh. I also have sensitive parts where your bony pubic bone hits - ouch! But too much of a belly and I have trouble getting aroused (have you seen you?) and I can't get my hips at the right angle with a big belly in the way if you know what I mean.

Line of sight concept when it comes to men's happy bits...if you can't see em we don't want to. We do take in the surroundings you know. We are not as visual as men but we do have eyes. Crawl across your bed naked while looking in a mirror. That is what is coming at us. I'm almost fifty years old over here; I'm trying to stay wet! Can you help a girl out? Do you look sexy to you? Pregnant? Pendulous moobs? Oh God make it stop!

That's how you are coming at us. Does it make your vagina slam shut too? I'm just trying to raise awareness. On the subject of man boobs - I'm not feeling the slightest bit attracted to breasts. At least keep them covered in hair so that I can ignore them more easily. I love hairy chests! Mm mm just want to lay my face on your soft chest. I don't want a man trying to look like a little boy. Let's all look like grown ups and have lots of sex!

Men should be mad about high-fructose corn syrup, preservatives and pesticides. These chemicals are helping make it hard to control your fat. It is alcohol that makes men look pregnant though. That one is not that hard to figure out. Could men please get pissed off about how chemical companies have hijacked our food system? That chicken you are eating bears a resemblance to a real chicken only in name. There is plenty of food for everyone, so stop using starving people as an excuse to poison us. Women can't even get paid maternity leave in the U.S. Let alone take on Monsanto. We need men so very bad to dive in on our industrial food!

When I watch TV, sometimes I just sit and wonder what the dude's dicks look like. How does it feel to be reduced to a part? Don't even pretend we think about your balls. We don't. This dick thinking is a new development on my part. Probably because I haven't seen any actual ones this year (ok, in truth, a lot of droopy old ones against my will at work – pass me the brain-bleach please) "excuse me sir, could you move your balls to the left so that I can X-ray your knee?" Gravity is our mutual enemy.

I was looking for more information on how man are doing these days on askmen.com and found the top story was "ten embarrassing that will get you laughed out of the bedroom". It's a funny list from "Bad advice guy". Who I myself would sleep with (based on what he looks like), any man who can be that open about trying to make a woman happy is for me. I have never heard of a woman kicking a man out of the bedroom. Is that a thing now? Why would you want a woman who only wants you for your sex skills? Who the hell do you think we are? Oh wait...

In one of the favorite relationships of my life, standard sex was: he came first then I got a bunch of orgasms before he got his second one. It was great! No pressure on anyone.

Hey feminists, I found some fringing equality! Drugs, cheating and domestic violence are all about half men and half women. Who knew? So if women are not living like innocent victims then will video games start to include female pixels that have their own story lines? More importantly, can all support agencies take on helping men AND women right now please? I know that men make more money so generally they can afford to purchase help more often then women can. I don't think we can assume this is always the case. Do we even know how much need there is? Statistically it should be equal. There is very little help out there for men for domestic abuse. Ok there is almost none to be more accurate. This kind of weird quiet discrimination seems to be a big part of what men don't want to talk about. Like you are less of a man because you were raised not to hit women and your wife just beat the crap out of you. Where do you go? If an agency takes money from the public in any way to help families affected by domestic violence then they should help any family. It is ridiculous that they don't. It is worse then ridiculous, it is criminal. If two grown ups want to live with violence I don't really care. If there are kids involved, then damage is being done that is morally wrong and costs all of the rest of us more money down the line, not to mention the trauma to innocent children.

I'm worried about the advice women of my generation have been getting for years: that we need to be very careful in how we talk to our males. We need to be always taking into account what kind of mother he had and always, above all, remember that he's just a little boy inside who's feeling are easily hurt. Ok shouldn't we take others feelings into account in general? Is it really appropriate in every day life to expect another human to take on your entire, possible horrible, past? Here is a test you can use to see if advice is fair: men, if you want to have a happy marriage you must always respectfully communicate with your woman and remember that she's just a little girl inside who's feelings are easily hurt. That sounds fair to me.

Why does it kind of feel wrong? Kind of like offering dudes beads

for flashing their dicks (you would be out of beads fast!).

Men are not required to be emotionally mature in our culture. I think

they used to be? My dad was not but really, neither is my mom in

many ways. What are the chances that I am?(poor) I am trying is all

I can say but I really resent the expectation that I have to

automatically treat all men like children and be their mom. I don't

want a dad just because mine was less then great in some ways. This

was probably due to his fatal flaw of just being a regular person

bumbling around the best he could just like all people (women

included). I cannot reconcile in my head that a man wants time to be

a protector but I have to care for him like a child. I don't want any

sexy time with a child! (Well Evan Peters is hot but chances are I will

never meet him...on second thought no chest hair. Boo.)

Is it fair of me to go into a relationship and not inform the man that I

will never, ever be interested in "Fifty Shade of Grey" style play

because I've actually been raped it's not arousing, it's terrifying and I need for sex to be a safe place. I have done the work on my self to reclaim my sexuality and I really love sex now with this one small caveat. I sure as hell don't think it's someone else's job to make all my past hurts better! I think it's hard to make huge generalizations about people because we are all different. I realize that people change and that the guys that raped me are probably not still running around raping people. Are they married with daughters? Should they have at least received a tattoo to warn others? Whenever married men ask for my number I give it to them...in black sharpie marker on their arm. I know it's shocking that anyone asks me since I'm "over the wall".

There is still a pervasive attitude in our culture that women are responsible for men on top of literally everything else. Women need to learn to share the load even though many will feel crazy guilty about asking for help and will micromanage the helper. Men are awesome and powerful and needed. Not just for the many millions of single parents living in poverty. At least most of us are putting our kids before ourselves, which is more, then I can say about most noncustodial parents. Yes, right now the Aerosmith song "Jaded" is playing in my head.

I sometimes wonder if children are so often born into difficult situations because you don't learn anything in life when things are going good. Working through adversity you can learn a million lessons about love, survival and priorities. If you never face any challenges, you never learn that you can accomplish things. Can we put some of these lessons in video games and still make them awesome? I bet we can, games are designed by some of the most brilliant people in our society. Would "get a job in the real world" be a good game? Degrees of difficulty added if you have those flappy holes from having gauges. You would have to do some kind of training, make a budget and find an apartment. You could get thrown in jail etc.

Many husbands that I know is to one extent or another is like another child for their wives to take care of. Many wouldn't be able to finish my game. I am pretty sure they all had their own underwear when they were dating - ladies I suggest you find out who bought his undies before you marry him. If it was his mom, you are next. Who wants to have sex with a child? Don't answer that.

More research on men and games led me to Anita Sarkeesian. The male gaming community hates her. There is even a game where you can beat her up.

I just watched all the videos I could find on Anita Sarkeesian. I wish she had been around when I was growing up. She used a great quote by Katha Pollit in the New York Times April 7, 1991 "Hers; the Smurfette Principle, The message is clear. Boys are the norm, girls the variation; boys are central, girls peripheral; boys are individuals, girls types. Boys define the group; it's story and its code of values. Girls exist only in relation to boys."

That last line really describes my childhood! My parent's first two children were "non-boys" but we still played with trucks. Our family didn't have much money, in fact my mom always made more then my dad but I was over thirty years old when I learned this fact. I had two dolls if you can imagine. Not even a Barbie - a Miss America doll with pose-able hair and the little sister doll. Uh oh, existential crisis. Apparently I have we been watching too much Danisnotonfire? (On YouTube)

So male is the norm and female is a deviation from the norm. In video games Sarkeesian points out the female character is often the only female in the otherwise male world. In the real world we are about even in terms of males and females. I love that Anita Sarkeesian exists. She is the most articulate woman I have ever seen. I would respectfully like to suggest, that her message would go further if she used more commonly used language in describing her very good points. I like to think that I have a good vocabulary (it gets better when I'm angry) but I needed to look up many words. I only have a Bachelors degree and can't afford a Masters so perhaps I'm just jealous.

Many video games say that it is ok or required for boys to kill things, especially sexy women. Will some men get "gamer PTSD" and have to fight the urge to kill women in real life. Probably not but...oh wait, it's already happening a lot (at least abuse if not murder) whether or not video games are to blame. I wonder if women were given the same chance to blow away some douche-bag men in video games that we would love it! Extra points! Oh yeah! See now am I bad? What about being able to punch a dude that cries just to get his own way? Yes, that happens. What about a hunt the rapist game? Hunt the pedophiles? Hunt the drug dealer selling at the elementary school? Hunt the deadbeat non-custodial parent? I guess I want to blow stuff up too. What does a female hero look like? Can she have a better outfit then tights and a cape? Wait why do dude superheroes wear tights? How did that ever start?

I think as games become more complex, all of the characters will become more interesting. There are probably people who write video games that are so smart that they could let you see life through the eyes of a crazy cat lady and make it interesting.

It seems like what happened with video games was that boys started gaming earlier and more aggressively then girls did because girls would rather talk then click. So naturally gaming companies catered to the kids saving up their money to buy games. If it had been girls first, games would be very different. Now that girls want to spend money on games, games will be made that cater to them. I don't think we should get too crazy assuming prejudice when it's just the dollar that says what games get produced.

Perhaps a few games that are the exact sexual reverse of existing games would be fun.

4 QUANTUM ENTANGLEMENT (POSSIBLE SOLUTIONS)

Things keep getting in the way of the fact that all adults have the

"Urge to merge" as Martha Beck says (love her). Can men and

women come together so that we can all have happy sexy lives? Let's

kill the forces driving us apart! We are meant to play together. Here

is a one hundred year old warning:

"Look back at history. Look at any great system of ethics, from the

Orient up. Didn't they all preach the sacrifice of personal joy?

Under all the complications of verbiage, haven't they all had a single

leitmotif: sacrifice, renunciation, and self-denial? Haven't you been

able to catch their theme song - 'Give up, give up, give up, give up'?

Look at the moral atmosphere of today. Everything enjoyable, from

cigarettes to sex to ambition to the profit motive, is considered

depraved or sinful. Just prove that a thing makes men happy - and you've damned it. That's how far we've come. We've tied happiness

to guilt. And we've got mankind by the throat." More ..."Every

system of ethics that preached sacrifice grew into a world power and

ruled millions of men. Of course, you must dress it up. You must

tell people that they'll achieve a superior kind of happiness by giving

up everything that makes them happy. You don't have to be to clear

about it. Use big vague words. 'Universal Harmony' - 'Eternal Spirit'

- 'Divine Purpose' - 'Nirvana' - 'Paradise' - 'Racial Supremacy' - 'The

Dictatorship of the Proletariat.' Internal corruption, Peter. That's

the oldest one of all. The farce has been going on for centuries and

men still fall for it. Yet the test should be so simple: just listen to any

prophet and if you hear him speak of sacrifice - run." Ayn Rand *The*

Fountainhead Centennial Edition.

To love is to value. Someone who tells you that you can love without

value is someone who will tell you that you can grow rich by

consuming. Oh and aren't we consuming! But think about this:

every piece of plastic that we ever made still exists. Nature has not

found a way to clean up our mess. We have to do it. There is a

plastic island in the Pacific Ocean bigger then some states. Should we send all of our plastic there, fuse it together somehow and build

on it? Then stop producing so much plastic that doesn't break

down? That was way too much seriousness! I'm sorry, I get excited.

Ok enough of me trying to impress you with how deep I can be.

How about a real, practical solution? Putting the toilet seat down.

As a chick I never want to touch it. Not ever, I don't even like

cleaning the toilet (who does? If men did it they would get combat

pay). Stay with me, I have a two-pronged (ha pronged) solution:

new, self-cleaning, heated seat toilets with no stupid flimsy seat that

goes up and down. Let's give men really cool urinals with built-in

video games where you get points for aim. Potty training ease! Pee

on Mario or whoever you want (extra fancy upgrade could be the

political candidate option or your boss. Send a pic from your phone

of your boss and pee away right in his or her face! Feel a little

better?). These would need to be self-cleaning too. Life could be so

much better! If you have an expensive house with an old boring

toilet and bidet option there should be an easy upgrade since the

plumbing is already there! No more nasty seat that even goes up and

down! No more nasty thing that no one wants to touch.

Ok, most builders are men so I have to ask the question "why do builders put toilets and bathtubs so close together?" Probably plumbing but does it have to be that way? It's awful. I can't relax in a tub next to an icky toilet. Oh, builders probably don't take baths. Kids and chicks do. There must be a better way! Maybe I just don't know about it. I've never had the privilege of a garage or a toilet that was more then two feet from the tub.

So when women are married they don't live as long but married men live longer. Hmm I think it's because women are taking care of them and it wears the women out. We like sex too if we are not exhausted and if that's not the only time you touch us. On sex: I would just want the right of first refusal in my marriage vows should I ever make any. I would simply ask that my husband ask me for sex first. If I refuse what he wants then he should be free to buy it from a professional in a safe, clean, professional manner. It should be the same for women. Sometimes we don't need or can't handle an emotionally charged exchange, its just sex sometimes. I think we will look back on these days when prostitution was illegal with the disgust we now apply to back alley abortions. The current plan is childish, unsafe, deadly and a waste of police time. Government needs to stay out of our private parts.

Legalize prostitution.

Webster's Dictionary: "The act or practice of indulging in promiscuous sexual relationships in exchange for money." So I guess I know some marriages that should be renamed. Ladies, if you only have one client, you are still a prostitute. If you are only with someone for the money don't pretend it's something that it's not. From what I've read, women only relatively recently (historically) got to own their own clothes so I am hoping that soon we will own our own bodies to do with as we please. A big part of keeping prostitution illegal is to deny the rights of women under the guise of protecting us. Laws against it have not stopped or slowed it or had any effect on women brought into this country to be nothing but sex slaves. Are we afraid these women will work their way out of poverty? We are the only ones raising kids most of the time, why are you making it harder for women to better themselves? Are men afraid that prices will go up and that if prostitutes are safer you won't be able to get off by beating and raping them?

Let's thinks this through. Right now most prostitutes are: on drugs, beaten regularly, of human slaves, arrested occasionally, at risk constantly of health problems and discarded when they are worn out. Would you want that life for your child? Why do men tolerate this? They are funding it. What mind-fuck makes you think this is ok?

What could we have if we tried? Barbershop & Blowjob? Watch out Starbucks! Multiple outlets for anyone's sexual needs would be nice. Would it be easier to find someone that is truly good for us if we have another option for sex? If a prostitute does it for you, don't be pretending that you love a girl just for sex. Have some integrity with yourself. Is marriage supposed to be more about love sex or control? I vote love and trust. Home needs to be protected and defended as a safe place to be you. If one spouse is frustrated because, for some reason, the other can't have sex shouldn't there be a healthy safe alternative that isn't criminal? If I really love someone, I don't want him or her to be forced into abstinence because my plumbing is broken. It is so crazy that sex is controlled by our government (who wants to keep us fighting about abortion so we don't see how sick they really are). How did this even happen? Fucking Puritans. The

Catholic Church was probably worried that they would lose control of people if they were allowed to enjoy their lives. The more miserable our lives, the more we need religious help and pharmaceutical intervention. They (drug companies and government) would break us more if they could because there is so much money in keeping us weak, fighting with each other and unhappy. We have toxic food, chemicals polluting everything, antibiotics killing our natural defenses. All other organized governments are doing a better job at protecting their people's health then the US.

What if this one change in our culture of making sex much less taboo dropped the rate of rape and molestation of young boys and girls by half? Wouldn't it be worth a try? Sex really is ok and good for you. There are no bad parts of your body. Stop shaming people about their natural tendencies. Catholic Church I'm talking to you. I'm sure we can come up with a religious discount to make the change easier. (I had to put that I there because I may not have pissed off enough people yet.)

Can we call them specialties instead of fetishes? It just sounds better. Can we women please have some porn that makes sense to us? Are there any chick directors in porn? We don't want to see dangling stuff. I know the pudgy dad body is now in style but come on. How about hot guys loving some mom-bodies? I haven't seen many but the ones that I have seen include ugly dudes with dicks way too big for real life. I feel sorry for the women they are with as they pretend to enjoy themselves.

Caution, Whining: the other kids are doing it: www.psu.edu/wmst

"In 1949, the United Nations adopted a resolution in favor of the decriminalization of prostitution, which has been ratified by 50 countries."

Prostitute Education Network: "The average age of someone entering into prostitution is 14 years. At least 75% of prostitutes were sexually and physically abused as children. The majority of prostitutes become addicted to alcohol or drugs. The National Task Force on prostitution suggests that over one million people in the US have worked as prostitutes. Estimates in some larger cities found that 20-30% of prostitutes are male. There is a lot of abuse of prostitutes - they get raped a lot - 5% of the time by cops with badges. Many prostitutes are suicidal and don't take care of themselves. 70% of adult men have engaged in prostitution at least once. Average prostitution arrests include 70% females, 20% males and 10% customers. 85-90% of those arrested work on the street." I bet there is actually a lot more prostitution. I hope some of it is nice and safe. In the US we arrest the prostitute instead of the client. This has not worked in the many years we have been doing it. Other countries arrest the customers and they are finding the strategy more effective.

"Cities spend an average of 7.5 million dollars up to 23 million on prostitution control every year. In the US that equals a 14.5 billion dollar a year business. Can we make the working people healthier? Wouldn't it indirectly make the people they serve safer? Can sanity win out over Puritanism or whatever it is that keeps it as a crime? It is happening anyway are we handling this in the most loving way possible? Would we really be less safe if prostitutes were independent contractors? Who exactly are we "keeping safe" here? Who is making the most money off of prostitution? Police? Pimps? I know it's not the sex workers who start at 14 years old and are discarded by age 20.

Make the places for sex like spas. I myself have not had sex in over a year and it's making me really cranky. I think chicks in their 40's would be all about it too. I seriously think that there should be sex therapists that help people work through things...no, it is not ok that you can't get off unless you are watching women be hacked to pieces. Go see someone you sicko. I hope that Kim Kardashian is more then just her rear end. When women are striving to be people not just parts, the hubbub over her butt tells me that we have a long ways to go. I would like way more people to be happy, healthy people.

Legalize Pot, and maybe the rest of drugs

www.drugwaracts.org. "Netherlands drug policy: Police and Public Prosecutor give low priority to the investigation of possession of small amounts of a drug for own use. The Opium Act Directive of the Public Prosecutor state that, if the offense concerns possession of small amounts for own use of a hard drug, the drugs will be seized, but normally there will be no custody or prosecution. Diversion to care is the primary aim of custody or prosecution in cases of

possession of hard drugs (Directive Opium Act 2011 A021 2012,

www.om.nl) 'small amounts' of a hard drug are defined as one tablet,

ampule, wrapple or ball of the drug and in many case an amount no

more than 0.5 grams. With regard to cannabis (categorized as a 'soft

drug') small amounts are defined as no more that 5 grams and no

more than 5 cannabis plants (stc. 2011-22936). Sounds like the

Netherlands are able to make rules that make sense - could we learn

from them? How many more generations of organized crime and

gang violence do we need to enjoy before we try something else?

Mostly men go to jail for drugs even though I'm sure equal numbers

of men and women actually DO drugs. I think it would mainly help

men to legalize pot. It seems silly for me to make that case here.

There is an excellent Ted Talk covering this exact topic. I think it is

just a question of how and when.

How much of an improvement makes it worth changing? If even 20

percent more men were surrounded by help and love, or whatever

makes them happy it would save us approximately how much per year? What would that do to the US economy? The local economy? Could we then look at reducing the size of the prison system (please don't kill me prison people)? Let's scrape off the top 5 percent of first time drug users arrested and put them through some serious rehab/job training/parenting classes. It has to be cheaper then the 30k per year we are paying now. We could be strict and triple their sentence if they are ever arrested again after that. If you are turning to hard drugs I think you are really committing the stupidest form of suicide. Can we just call it that? Do you really think you will ever be ok again after doing meth? You are at the least going to need some major help. Any help that we give these people will be cheaper for us then keeping them in prison. Are these people really a danger? Who does it help when they are locked up at a huge financial burden to us? We are putting ridiculous numbers of men behind bars – something needs to change!

Notes from book "Men on Strike" by Helen Smith PhD
"I propose that men are autonomous beings who are entitled to justice and equality and the pursuit of their own happiness because they are human beings in a supposedly free society." Yes, let's do

that! More from her: "I wonder how much the demonization of men leads to our staggering male suicide rate? Men kill themselves at much higher rates then women. It's politically correct to laugh at men, beat them or hurl insults their way. Most men don't say anything and just retreat to the basement to tune out the world, and who can blame them? A wounded animal retreats to its cave and now America's men are doing the same thing down in their 'man caves'. Yes it's nice that men at least have some place in the house to call their own. However, the man-cave is really no more then a booby-prize for men who must swallow their manhood and head downstairs in order to get some peace and hope that womenfolk and the government stay out of their way." Are you fucking serious lady? They are hiding from doing chores! Where is the special woman's room? The kitchen? She had me on her side up to the man cave stuff.

More Men on Strike (I'm trying to understand other viewpoints by reading things that I don't agree with)

"...But do we really want to live in a women-and-children-last world? I don't think that many men would really be happy with that either.

A better solution is for men to retain their male virtues but learn to speak up for themselves when needed. Society - or at least parts of society that cater to women - May not like that, but it is a change our society needs to make. Maybe when there are no more men working, people will start to notice, until then, they will just continue to discuss the 'war on women' until there are no more men anywhere. Maybe that is what feminists wanted all along. One thing is clear, if women were dropping out of the workforce at this rate, it would be considered a national crisis. But if men do it, there is hardly a whimper, because no one is listening." So women should go live off the system on disability and in jail like men? I don't really get what Helen is trying to say but I don't see anything in her book about making men accountable for their own choices.

Ok, she makes me kind of mad but here's more: "Men as a whole want to be doing things and taking risks that lead to innovation and economic growth, not hanging out all the time in the basement without purpose." "You know the saying, 'If mamma ain't happy, ain't nobody happy'. Well it's not true. Your happiness matters too. Don't be an emotional hostage; start speaking up to your significant other about issues that concern you. Quit hiding in the basement with a beer and swallowing your anger or hurt over something she said." "Professor Higdon discussed the idea of coverture that now, he says, pertains to men instead of women. Coverture was part of common law in England and the United States throughout the nineteenth century and was legal doctrine 'whereby, upon marriage, a woman's legal rights were subsumed by those of her husband." Ok but men still often have economic control over their domestic situations. That, right there, is a big part of why my policy on marriage has historically been "just say no". She does go on (Helen has a lot of hate): "White knights and Uncle Tims are both types of men who elevate women to a privileged position in different ways, often for different reasons. The white knight wants to take care of women and sees her as a damsel in distress who needs masculine protection to get by. An Uncle Tim is generally a sellout to his own gender who is more then likely either a politician type - usually liberal - or just a guy trying to get laid who thinks his PC behavior will get him laid more often. Point this out as frequently as possible and make fun of him for it. Shaming him is vital." Wow so being nice to women at all is bad to Mrs. Smith...? She seems to want men to speak for themselves but if they are "woman positive" in any way we should shame them? She looks like a female in her picture. I don't think that hate solves anything but it can close your eyes to opinions other then your own.

"Men are terrified of angry, judgmental women. So, no matter how weird or disturbing you think of what your boyfriend or husband says, listen and don't interrupt with how he <u>should</u> feel. Just let him talk. At the same time, don't try to get him to talk about your relationship constantly; this is a relationship killer." I'm a chick and I'd rather do anything other then talk about my feelings. People are individuals. Women are already busy doing everything, dudes need to get it together and be responsible for something. At the very least take on your own choices.

"Our society is made better by men who are productive, happy and treated with fairness. We have only ourselves to blame if we do not turn the tide on the war on men, for without half the human experience, our society can crumble, just as surely as those New York buildings would if they no longer had men to work their sublime

male poetry on them. Is that the world you want to live in? I don't."
Ok I agree with Helen Smith there. Men are amazing, strong and
beautiful. I truly believe they can have and be so much more then
they allow.

I am confused; men negotiate their salaries but not the rest of their
lives? Many women (me included) can't negotiate about money but
we can talk about anything else. Derp! Boy do we need each other!
Males and females have different strengths and skills neither are
better or more valuable for the last couple hundred years. How do
we signal to boys that they are now men? Girls bleed when they are
old enough. I think all kids could benefit from a better transition.

Coming of Age Day - Japan holiday held annually on the second
Monday of January. It is held to congratulate all those who have
reached the age of majority (twenty years old) over the last year to
help them realize that they have become adults. Began in 714 AD
source Wikipedia 12/5/2014 (so my source may be just made up but
I like it). Could we do something like this on Eric Kyle Day? I think
the American Sniper is soon to have his own day and it seems a

fitting day to celebrate all of those people coming of age in the
United States. I guess it would need to be 18 since that's the age
where we send people to war. I would hope it would be more then
just drunkenness. What is the appropriate symbol for such an
occasion? Could we use a very specific tattoo that you can only get
on your 18th birthday in a specific design? I love micro-tattoos!
They say to me that it is more of a reminder to you then for showing
off to others. I think a tiny crown with the year you turn eighteen
would be fun.

When have we taught men that it's ok to feel? Can they have feelings
at the football game? When else? Are there any times at all when its
ok for men to show their feelings that are not sports related? Oh yes,
funerals but only sometimes - not really. In all of life that's all that
you guys are willing to negotiate for? I have seen some men cry at
the births of their children. Can we gradually draw a bigger circle of
emotions that men are allowed to have so they stop blowing up and
killing their families and then themselves. I know most women
would be ok with it but it is other men that are the problem. Men are
the architects and enforcers of their own cages.

Let's allow boys to have emotions at any age. Not just showing

strength - but all of the emotions. The best teams of any kind are

when males and females can work together. You can get the

strengths of both. Especially in investing. It has been proven many

times that investing groups made up of equal amounts of man and

women perform the best if both parties have equal say in decisions.

Women tend to hold stocks too long and men tend to dump them

too quickly. Groups of women and men working together perform

best.

When do we need to start making some changes? What is our

breaking point to make some real changes? How about a mass

suicide at some high school that hooked up with a Jim Jones type

person? Let's think about school shootings all of them have been

done by males. It started Feb. 19, 1997 with Evan Ramsey, sixteen

years old, a junior at Bethel Regional High in Bethel, Alaska. Two

people were killed and two were injured. Evan is in jail for two

ninety-nine year sentences and is eligible for parole in 2060. His Dad

blames the video game Doom according to Wikipedia. Other kids

learned from this and replicated their actions. The shootings keep
getting worse; I'm not sure where it will end. So um, way before age
sixteen would be a great place to start. I think we get the point that
kids will kill their peers for fame, even if it means killing themselves.
No one is paying any attention to these kids or spending time with
them so they feel they have no value. I get that. I guess it's good I
directed my destruction at myself in high school and not at others.
These kids can't see a future for themselves - that is our fault for
taking them out of the world and putting them in a box to learn
things are not useful to 90 percent of them. The light seems to go
out of their eyes in fifth grade. Do we really need that many poorly
trained secretaries? Even if men start feeling and openly expressing
their emotions I promise they will still be fundamentally different
from women.

The 1990s and 2000s saw little boys in schools treated like pre-rapists
and pre-violent people. Perhaps if we stop assuming they are bad
and stop trying to turn them into girls (yes we really have been doing
that) and play to their strengths, we will stop making them so bored,
frustrated and entitled that they want to kill people. Do they have

value to us or not? Teach boys to respect themselves and respect women. I think these two thing are very closely linked. Unless you have actually done all the things required to keep a house clean for example, you naturally think it must be easy. I assume engineering is easy. Shows how little I know about Engineering right? Programming must be an absolute piece of cake.

School stuff that has been proven to work: same sex classes (yes, I said that) especially in English for boys and math for girls. Doing something that is hard for you is even harder to do in front of someone you may have a crush on. Let's make sure the teachers and students are not wasted on drugs or alcohol. I think school times need to be flexible and between 8:30 am and 5:30 pm. Lunches need to be an hour long so kids can eat, play or nap. In Sweden kids get two hours for lunch – I know this because my daughter looked it up. This will help them pay attention. We used to give kids the summers off so that kids could help bring in the crops. I wasn't there but I'm pretty sure those kids would have rather been in school then working in the most dangerous profession. Our kids know nothing of working in the field for fourteen hours at a stretch. We used to make kids work like adults too soon. Now we do it way too late.

I feel very strongly that some stuff about school needs to change. You may want to skip ahead. How have we now gone to a schedule that makes it impossible for parents to work and keep their kids safe? I don't care who did it, we need to fix it. High school needs to end at 16 years old. Vocational internships need to start then. No they are not people yet but they are not helpless children either. They are old enough to try their hand at a real job. We need a few common sense rules to make it work of course.

 I don't want to go back to the days when the owner of the sweatshop also owned the orphanage.

There are lots of jobs in research and development that a 16 year old could do. You have to let them sleep though. Many of them, especially boys, are not done growing yet. Can we please focus our efforts on producing functional, self-supporting adults? I'm not sure what the hell we are doing now but the outcomes are clearly not the best we can do for anyone involved. Kids know their time is being wasted. We should listen to them and implement solutions that meet broader goals then passing some weird test that has zero reliability for correlating with being a successful self-supporting adult. Every teacher that I know and love wants to see kids succeed so bad that they have given their lives over to the task. Then there are teaches that are drunk or high at work and the administrators and unions that make sure that their jobs are protected. They are accessories to the crime of wasting our kids.

Every time you do something for your child (instead of letting them do it themselves), you are sending them the message that you don't think they can do it themselves. I'm talking to you moms. I am fighting this battle with my daughter right now. The fear of the unknown is really always worse then he actual thing. If we never demand that our kids try then they never get past the fear and learn that they are capable. Teens need to be able to make some mistakes. Parents could go with their kids to a money management class. Let the kids pay bills for once so that they will understand what they are up against when they are on their own. See what choices they want to make. Isn't it better for them to practice before they really fall on their faces? Right now we boot them out into the world and the financial services industry is happy to make billions of interest off of our kids learning financial lessons the hard way. Please don't kill me banking people.

It would be good to show these kids that we need them before they get that tossed away feeling?

I think it's clear that it's not ok for both parents to work full-time because it allows no time for someone to raise the children. I think it's also clear that government in any form is not a good alternative. We are sliding that way and it sucks for kids. Children know when work and money come before them and it makes them feel that they have no value. They are just trying to figure things out. I know that their parents love them but it is not translating into their kids. There is just no real way to make up for being there. Kids don't need quality time they need actual time.

There is a book out "Do Fathers Matter, what science is telling us about the parent we've overlooked" by Paul Raeburn. Spoiler alert...they do matter, very much in fact. The fact that we need men

to show that they care about children is my main motivation for

trying to start trouble with this book.

Back to Raeburn's book: The book gives scientific evidence that

fathers are vital to a child's development. It's about time. It is really

hard being a mom and dad most of the time (and home repairs ugh).

I love that my daughter's dad wants to be in her life but we

communicate very poorly. So most of the year, at least in person, I'm

all my daughter has. I wish her Dad hadn't moved two states away.

If he lived closer, he could be there for her. Kids need to really know

both of their parents.

If you judge parenting as readying your child to take care of itself

then I wouldn't say we are doing the best job we can. Here is some

info to get your attention: Bloomberg Business Week January 12,

2015 "80% - Share of college-age Cubans enrolled in post secondary

education." We are a bit behind at about 30 percent. Is college the

answer to everything's? Heck no, but generally we aren't giving children that are not bound for college any useful life skills let alone job training. Can we at least give them a fighting chance? A fourth-grade child can be taught to balance a checkbook. Why are we paying so much for years of algebra? Ok, if there has to be so much algebra then let there be life skills too (money basics, self care, car care, home care - let local companies use it for advertising). And before I quit preaching...hey schools...take a cue from medicine and first do no harm. Let them sleep and eat. No you are not, stop lying to yourself. My kid has 30 minutes for lunches - and has for years. What this means is get your lunch, line up, walk to the cafeteria (10 min are gone), stand in line if you didn't bring lunch, eat, clean up, line up walk back to your classroom. Actual eating time is about 10 minutes. God help you if you can't get your pudding open!

Sorry for another massive tangent! Back to dudes…"In her book, The War Against Boys, Sommers explains in detail the efforts of "feminists and their sycophants" to turn the educational system into one that favors girls at the expense of boys. Boys and their masculine traits and needs are often frowned upon in US schools, and boys are now seen as 'defective girls' in need of a major overhaul." "...The belief that boys are being wrongly 'masculinized' is inspiring a movement to 'construct boyhood in ways that will render boys less competitive, more emotionally expressive, more nurturing - more in short, like girls."

Could we instead rejoice that they are boys with special strengths that they can use to have a great life? We need more men involved in schools to stop the crap that boys are putting up with! If you don't think it's there, check it out! I don't know how but we need to get kids some opportunities that are not linked to their sex. What if a boy wants to be a chef? What if a girl wants to fix cars (actually their hands are smaller to fit in little places - this is also why they can be better surgeons)?

I love teachers. I think they are some of the greatest and smartest people we have and they reach out to our kids with their giant hearts. What more could you ask of a teacher? Then we dump them in a horrible plan of destruction and don't give them the resources they need or protect them from crazy parents. They are also inundated with children that have severe barriers to learning. We are making it really hard for them to teach kids. It's just so horrible and a big ugly sleep deprived plan that it's really hard to unravel. Stop wasting all these great teachers on a messed up system! Clearly their union is hopelessly lost as far as purpose goes. The bigger an organization is, the more likely it is that their main mission will go astray. It seems like the children don't have an advocate in the current system.

Christina Hoff Sommers: "The moment a young man arrives on the college campus, he is treated as a member of a suspect class. One popular freshman orientation program is called 'She Fears You'. Next there are 'Take Back the Night' marches, performances of the vagina monologues - accusing posters plastered all around the school - and lots of classroom readings - all driving home the point that women are from Venus and men are from hell." What guy would want to go to class in that environment? I bet some men start out believing that they will be different - non-attackers and end up tired and bitter at fighting something they never started. Are we just telling them what we expect? Do they start to feel that they must be missing something if they are not raping women?

There is a new movie about campus rape "The Hunting Ground".

That should help. When you silence hurt people, eventually their story is going to come out. It sounds like colleges should not be in the business of judging what is fair in any assault. Why is sexual assault different? Take all responsibilities for acting as a judicial entity away from schools. Clearly they are screwing it up and providing justice for no one. Who let them have that power in the first place? Doh! Colleges should not be above the law. Especially when they make more money (enroll more students) by saying they have a safe campus.

I need to go back to the vitality of men to kids because this stuff is pissing me off.

Exactly how important are men in parenting? When men become parents, if they are living with the mother, men's bodies make some major changes in response to a women's increased estrogen levels during pregnancy. So if men's bodies, hormones, and emotions change during their partner's pregnancies, most notably: "In a study by Story and Wynne-Edwards found that men's testosterone levels fell 35 percent when they had their first contact with their babies compared to measurements taken near the end of their wives pregnancies." There must be a reason men's actual physiology changes from the minute they make a baby if they stick around. Do men who stick around live longer? Do the kids?

In the Book "Do Fathers Matter "When we rid ourselves of the things we think we know about fathers, and replace them with what we are now learning, we can do more to encourage fathers to become more involved with their children." More. "Fathers brains are significantly changed by spending time with their infants in the first four months of their lives. Fathers clearly have important connections with their infants and they treat them differently then their mothers." You see, children need the skills learned from both parents to have the best chance at doing well in life. We have to stop thinking that women can just do it all. We can't and neither can men.

More from the book: "We are learning amazing things about both parents - they are both able to pick out the cries of their own babies in a crowded daycare." I thought that only moms could do this. Watch a crowd of moms talking. You will see that all of them with babies or even grown children will be unconsciously rocking back and forth even when they are not holding their babies. It happens at the grocery store too. It's my own observation but I think it's cute.

There are ongoing studies of fatherhood and parenting. Some by James P. Curley of Columbia, summary: "Some mice pups that are not properly groomed by their fathers have difficulty recognizing new objects and show detrimental changes in stress hormones. Licking pups by either parent can change pup mouse brains - they are a lot less sensitive to stress with lots of licking". Go lick your baby! Just kidding, go do the human equivalent. Actually animal parents lick their children's wounds because spit has human growth hormones in it to promote healing. It clears up zits too. (I know gross!).

Lee T. Gettler and Christopher W. Kuzawa of Northwestern University. "362 people in study 92% slept with their children and showed a significant decline in testosterone - compared to fathers that slept in a different room. "Fathers who are more involved with their children have a reduced risk of illness and mortality that might be explained by their lower testosterone levels." It's even good for you! Can we study how baby cuddling affects depression? We could start a business renting out baby cuddle time to sad people? Are we doing things backwards? What happens to men's hormone levels when they spend time away from their children? If things like testosterone change when a baby shows up, what happens when the baby is gone? Is there a male version of postpartum depression? I'm no Dr. But I bet yes. Men also need to mourn the loss of having their wives all to themselves. I think we vastly underestimate what is going on pheromone and hormone wise for everyone when a baby is born. I may be overthinking things but if it takes a male and female human to make a baby and support a baby...shouldn't we understand the hormones involved so that we can intervene if things go south? What about the older kids? How are they affected?

Is this still a book if I have more questions then answers?

More cool stuff about parenting: University of North Carolina, Lynn Vernon-Feagans and Nadya Pancsofar at College of New Jersey summary - "Fathers matter more to their children's language development then Mothers." So why are dads so rarely seen at school? Is this costing us our future competitive advantage as a nation? I bet the impact is even more dramatic for boys then for girls (but the study did not say that).

To bring even more to the party of cool effects we will get if men choose to fight their way into parenting...Sweden - Uppsala University - "a particularly stunning result: fathers reading to seven year old girls and asking sixteen-year old girls about school helped to prevent depression and other psychological ailments in the kids decades later." Ok, this one really doesn't seem that hard.

What I would like to suggest to women is that you need to be a person too. Not only a mother. I know it is so easy to lose yourself in giving everything to your children. As long as the baby is happy, you think that things are all good. We end up letting friendships and interests just slide away because the baby is the priority we shut ourselves down. I think mostly because we think we are supposed to put ourselves last. Is that the best thing for anyone in this equation? Is it how you would want your child to live? Let the men in. The baby's will live I promise.

And the beat goes on da da dum...(props to Marshall Mathers) Bruce

J. Ellis, University of Arizona. "Ellis quickly discovered that there

was something about fathers that gave them a unique roll in

regulating their daughter's development - especially their sexual

development - around the time of puberty. In a series of studies

beginning in 1999, he found that when girls had a warm relationship

with their fathers and spent a lot of time with them in the first seven

years of their lives, they had a reduced risk of early puberty, early

initiation of sex, and teen pregnancy." So daughters need time with

their fathers just as much as boys do.

Feldman, Ruth at Bar-Ian University in Israel.

"Besides revealing a vital biological connection between fathers and

their children, the study also suggested a novel way of treating

children with social disorders: treat their parents with oxytocin.

"Giving oxytocin to the parents of those children might deepen the

parent-child relationships that autism can disrupt. That change in

turn, could boost levels of oxytocin in children - and their ability to

interact socially with others."

Feldman and her group also discovered that "the hormone prolactin

has an important role to play for fathers and their children. As we saw earlier, prolactin, which is related to lactation in women, rises in fathers near the end of their partner's pregnancy and after birth. In men, prolactin is related to the way fathers play and their encouragement of children's desire to explore is itself characteristic of father play." The researchers speculated that as fathers become more familiar with their infants over time the prolactin and oxytocin systems create new connections between them. Both the emotional connection and the exploratory encouragement are key aspects of attachment between fathers and their children."

Yoda: "There is no try, do."

Women need to stop getting in the way of the interactions between fathers and children and controlling them. Men need to know they can do it and stop deferring to their wives. Leave it to men, they can figure it out in their own way. No one has ever proven fathers to be failures at raising children so why is it ok to treat them like they have already failed? What if you wanted to build something and they just wouldn't let you because they don't think you can do it. Would that be ok? No, we've gotten rid of lots of that for women in the last thirty years now it's time for kids to get the vast and important contributions that men hold for raising children better equipped to take care of and support themselves.

Of course, economics are important there will be less and less kids to play with...Demographics, Bloomberg Business Week December 22, 2014. "56% - The share of the recession's decline in births attributable to Hispanic women." "The latest recession left the U.S. With its lowest fertility rate on record." "According to the latest data from the National Center for Health Statistics, in 2013 they (fertile women) had just 62.5 babies, below the replacement rate. If this isn't a temporary blip associated with the weak economy, the American population will start to shrink." Why does this matter? Because there will be less and less people to work and pay for the people with their hands out. What do we do when the takers outnumber the givers? We need to think things through now. From another great book The Fountainhead by Ayn Rand "You can fake virtue for an audience. You can't fake it in your own eyes. Your ego is the strictest judge. They run from it. They spend their lives running. It's easier to donate a few thousand to charity and think oneself noble than to base self respect on personal standards of personal

achievement. It's simple to seek substitutes for competence - such

easy substitutes: love, charm, kindness, and charity. But there is no

substitute for competence." We are going to need competence from

every child in coming generations. To get that, we need both

parents.

According to Disney films, the worst possible thing that can happen

is for your mom to die. The entire killing of moms in movies has

become epidemic - it's not just Disney anymore it extends into teen

romance novels. Every teen novel: the girls all play acoustic guitar,

the boy says, "wow, you can really sing," girl says, "I haven't sung

since my mom died".   So kids have a tougher life living without

their mothers and are in the most peril. What about their dads? Why

are they automatically doomed without a mom? Can we get a better

narrative? All children's stories used to have a point, it seems like

there could be more then one theme. Is it some secret warning to

men? To women? Why are they killing us off? There are all sorts of

other useful lessons that kids need to learn. The stories of the old

days, before TV, came from your family and had a lesson - not to scare children about things that they can't control, like a parent dying and leaving them to fend for themselves. The news does it to us as adults. Our media has unending tales about death and horrible things. Generally, we can't do anything to help. This makes us feel powerless and sad. Do we want our kids to feel more powerless then they already do? Just being short and having bad manual dexterity should be enough.

From a comedian that I really like, Bill Burr as part of his performance "I'm So Sorry You Feel That Way", "Stop hugging your children, you are ruining this country! Ok, you got to hug your daughters, hug 'em right out of those hooker shoes. Let them know that you are a good man and they should find another one like you. Now your sons, you can hug em but every 3 or 4 you got to knock em down - come on, get up, it didn't hurt. My mom hugged me twice. Once when I was little and once when I moved out, because we thought we were supposed to. It was like two parking meters coming to life. Just awful." I think Mr. Burr would have benefitted from a couple more hugs early in life but he's hilarious.

A little bright spot in a whiny chapter:

The Ethics of American Youth Biennial Report on American Youth

by Josephson Institute of Ethics finds evidence that young people are

cheating, lying and stealing less. (Survey of 23,000 high school

students) "In 2010, 59% of students admitted they had cheated on

an exam in the past year, in 2012 that dropped to 51%. Lying to a

teacher about something significant dropped from 61% in 2010 to

55% in 2012. Those who lied to their parents about something

significant dropped from 80% to 76%." "93% of students said that

their parents or guardians want them to do the ethically right thing,

no matter the cost." "Boys are much more likely to harbor negative

attitudes and engage in dishonest conduct then girls." Not

surprising but why don't we figure out why we tolerate this from

boys? Do we just not care what boys do? To me, these figures seem

really high for our children. I'm glad they are getting better but they

are still bad across almost all measures!

Now, more reasons why we need to change: Unfit for Work, The

Startling Rise of Disability in America by Chana Joffe-Walt.

"Children (about 1.5M) are now on disability because they have learning problems. Some families live off the $700.00/mo. from one child with a learning disability." PCG Public Consulting Group will comb through your states welfare rolls and move as many people as possible to disability. PCG gets about $2,300 per person that they switch over.

 So you have your child supporting you because they have trouble learning. Do you want them to get better? Tough spot to be in! How can the fate and daily survival of an entire family rest on the shoulders of a seven-year-old? Ok, let's talk money for a minute.

What do men spend on sports vs. child support payments? I tried to find out but what I found was a list of the top five things that men spend money on from Investopedia Sept 23, 2011: Electronics, Alcohol, Cars, Gambling and last...sports. Can we move their kids into the top five? I think we need data from Dads – Dads are special people, you can't just lump tem together with all men.

From Fortified Financial: "Women spend money on: shopping (but while women may come home with a lot of shopping bags, the total cost of a women's shopping isn't even comparable to a man's number one spending choice), beauty, health and fitness, love/online dating and home furnishings."

Time is money so...I also found an American Time Use Survey Summary released June 18, 2014 so they are results from 2013. "On an average day, 83% of women and 65% of men spent some time doing household activities such as housework, cooking, lawn care or financial or other household management." But it also said, one the same page "on an average day, 19% of men did housework such as cleaning or doing laundry - compared to 49% of women Food prep 68%female, 42% men".

So it looks like they have time for parenting if they would make the choice to do it. What about some genetic evidence that they are needed? Got it!

From the great book "Do Father's Matter?" Quoting Haig's theory of competition in conception and pregnancy - he believes on the genetic level fathers and mothers compete for the limited resources available to the embryo in the womb - what genes that are essential for growth come from Mom vs. Dad and containing imprinted genes that encourage growth of the fetus from the mother - if the baby takes too much it could kill the mother (i.e. preeclampsia and diabetes) and the mother's counter weapons to preserve herself."

I don't actually agree with Haig on this. All of nature works in symbiotic relationships; I'm not clear on why it needs to be expressed as a battle. Later he says: "literally when you remove the controlling gene from females, the offspring grow too big and die before birth." He later states that these genes become dependent on each other for balance in the individual. "If you get a mutation in an imprinted gene, you get a really pathological outcome. One side lets go of the rope." Looking at how males and females are physically made, isn't it more likely that we each have copies of everything that is important to make a new person? I think I read somewhere (but I can't find the reference) that we may be able to cure some congenital issues by activating a gene copy that is "turned off". For example, the copy of a certain gene from mom is broken - so can we turn the one on from dad?

How long until we definitively link poisons in our food supply with congenital problems? Antibiotics? I won't go on and on about it here because I am not at all qualified (like I am qualified on anything) but I think we will soon look back with shame on these dark days of unregulated food producers and their factory animals. That's another book. Can we stop the huge and unfounded attack on vaccines? It's what you put in your face every day - not a shot you get once that is causing most of our expensive health problems.

Fathers are bringing more to the table then ever before but I don't think they are getting the respect they deserve. Single parent families are more common then two-parent families. This is sad to me and I'm one of them. The main people that make me angry are the men and women that have children then ignore them. Give them to someone that will take the time to enjoy them! Sorry that just makes me really angry. Go on with your selfishness; just leave the kids out of it. They are actual people – not a thing for you to use as leverage.

Unfortunately, some parents want parenting time to save or make money. They have no intention of spending time talking to their kids.

The greatest thing a Father can do is exactly the same as the greatest thing a Mother can do; share yourself, your time and your passions. It takes time to do that and the United States is the place where it is least likely to happen right now. Men and women should both get exactly the same time off to be with their children and we need for some of it to be paid or it can't happen. Do we want a next generation or not? Do you get that someone needs to raise the next generation of people? Do you get that it needs to be a smart choice to do so (read "not completely financially devastating"). Who do you think is going to work and pay into social security and other government programs?

There is a generation that grew up just not knowing our parents very well. Both of my parents always worked they never shared with me what they love about the world. They did complain about being stuck in jobs that they hated every day (but they tortured themselves for us - weird). So I grew up feeling guilty that they hated their lives. Why was it my fault that they choose the jobs they chose? My sister married a man like my dad and I am working where my mom worked for forty years. Not kidding, I am praying this book is my ticket out.

Here is a total tangent that shows the time crunch in our family: I will never forget when I got to go to "state" for track as a freshman in High School. I forgot my cleats and my Dad brought them to me before my race. It was great but he couldn't wait 15 minutes to see me race because he had to meet his coworker at the bar. He broke my heart that day. I have never felt more worthless. I knew I didn't want a man like that as a husband. I vowed to never do anything like that to my child.

A last parenting rant: Christmas - what a set up! Women do 95% of the work and give all the credit to a fat, fictional man. Nope, it was your mom, all your mom. Go give her a smooch now. When you see Christmas lights, here is the scam on that: if they were put up for free a woman put them up. If someone got paid, then a man put them up. This is part of why women have no time for anything extra around the holidays. Most of the women I know don't even bother to ask their husbands to help out at the holidays because, they know he will screw it up and they will just have to re-do it anyway. Are these women just control freaks or are their men just that incompetent? I'm not sure what the solution is here but it's definitely a problem. How did it get to be this way? Do women need to go on strike and act like men for the holidays one year so we can redefine the holidays to a celebration everyone can enjoy? Let's have an all-man Christmas where women do the parts men usually do, whatever they are. I know chicks will take the even years.

Both parents are working more hours. There are no two ways about what message that sends to your child, that they are not as important as money. It breaks their hearts, all of them. They will tell you it's ok then go do drugs because they feel like there is no way they can influence the situation without hurting their parents and yet they are separated. Raising your children means being there. I don't think it matters which parent is there, but hopefully it's the one that most wants to be. Because staying home with kids is way more difficult then any paid job. My daughter would come home from school and just sob because she was "holding it in all day". School is a bit of a break for parents but there is still a lot of work that goes into raising kids and taking care of a house. If they aren't sick from school, they forget stuff, then there are class parties and homework. Kids go through very different phases at school. They are learning to be social and that's not easy. They could be fine one day and not willing to let go of your leg the next (strong little buggers!). Am I supposed to call in kid-attached? If I were a boss, I would allow it or to come in as a set.

Men are not influencing their personal lives like they do their work lives:

"Ellen Galinsky and colleagues at the Families and work institute found that 'men experience more conflict between work and family then women' a surprising finding considering that most of the discussion about work and family has centered around women." In 2009 - 49% of men reported conflicts." So how many of these men have tried talking about their issues? Would there ever be a scenario where they could negotiate for better work/life balance?

"The US is the only country out of thirty leading democracies that does not have laws protecting workers paid maternity leave." Unpaid leave is only protected for half of jobs. Is it really necessary that we

have to choose between raising our kids in poverty and working?
How is it that we have the practices of a third-world sweatshop when
it comes to raising our kids?

"Schoppe-Sullivan found that mothers did play an important role in
both encouraging and curtailing father's involvement. And their
gatekeeping is a powerful force: even fathers who wanted to be
involved with their kids often drifted away in the face of persistent
maternal criticism. Encouragement clearly proved to have a more
powerful effect on fathers. Mothers can close the gate, but they can
also open the gate." Why do women make their lives more difficult
and less stable for them and their children by discouraging their
father's involvement? Someone should really study this and offer
solutions. I think part of it is women needing to be needed. Women
get sucked down a scary hole like Alice trying to be the perfect mom
and wife. This is impossible.

Do we really fundamentally distrust men? Do we feel like we need to
do everything because we have been let down? Is this they way we
want it to be? How can we change things so that men are engaged in

our society? I was raised in a strict Lutheran Church. At this church females were not allowed to be pastors or speak at church meetings. When I asked the pastor why he said it was "because if we let women speak they will do everything and men will not participate." So if I don't have a husband then I don't have a voice? Yep. Crazy! This policy takes away women's rights and assumes men are lazy children. How is that ok? Why are the churchmen ok with that plan unless they feel that women have no value?

What falls through the cracks...basically all the money for this little circus of raising children?

Total yearly WIC payments $6,899,608,031 FY budget 2014 - includes food grant and NSA grant. Best estimate of infants and children ages 1-4 at or below 185% of poverty 9.9 million total FY 2010. Source USDA www.fns.usda.gov The company that we used to do the study is Abt, a 50 year old company with a mission "To improve the quality of life and economic well being of people worldwide, it's personal to us." Has 10 unnamed outside directors. I have questions on why we don't alternate the people doing the study to make sure the results have not been compromised. Seems like they always get the same results. I think we are not getting the

information in a way that is helpful in setting public polices.

How do we finance this whole thing?

How prevalent is non-payment of child support? Louisiana - unpaid

in 2011: $1.2 billion, Texas unpaid in 2012 $11 billion, and total as of

Sept. 2006 according to aspe.hhs.gov was 105.4 billion nation wide.

These numbers are really hard to find and very difficult to assess

whether they are accurate. Child Support Lien Network 888-240-

7488, 31 states are members. "In 2013 the child support program

served 17 million children, nearly 1 in 4 children in the US. FY 2013

Office of Child Support Enforcement; Preliminary Report. LETS

JUST SAY THERE IS A LOT.

Is there so much unpaid support because men don't care or because

they are bitter at being pushed out of their children's lives? It is some

of both? We clearly need money to raise children but we need

fathers to be in their children's lives just as much. Whatever

happened in the adult relationship is never the child's fault but,

clearly now they are paying the price. Now and when the custodial parent is retired in poverty. Can we put any more pressure on kids? While non-custodial parents just party it up and feel sorry for themselves that they don't have more time with their kids.

It is mainly men that are making their own children pay the price. Everyone has heard stories of women who take money and buy themselves clothes instead of stuff for their children. I don't know who that one woman is but she needs to be stopped. When you give money to moms, it generally improves the out comes for their children in terms of health and diet. Stop believing the propaganda.

Thomas Sowell, The Quest for Cosmic Justice: "Within given families, there are performance differences on mental tests as between the first-born child and later children. A study of National Merit Scholarship finalists separated out the first-born from later siblings and discovered that more then half of these finalists were first-borns - even in five-child families. A later study showed that IQ differences among siblings translated into income differences between them of a multitude comparable to those between unrelated individuals with different IQs. If you cannot achieve equality of performance among people born to the same parents and raised under the same roof, how realistic is it to expect to achieve it across broader and deeper social divisions?"

It is harder then ever to make generalizations about the "average" family. We test kids to death to see how they are doing on some subjects but did we ever check to see if those subjects indeed lead to a better job or life? Can we just accept as fact that custodial parents need help and money?

I don't think the answer is all moms or all dads. But we need someone to do it, and I think it should be a benefit of employment. If you made it through that last little recession and still have a decent job, there should be some paid allowances made for raising your children. You bust your butt, graduate from training to do a good job and if you want to have a family you have to choose between poverty and not seeing your child. It's crap. Your employer says that you are their most valuable asset, unless you want to have kids. Employers: if you care about your people, let them care for their families.

I've seen people of all ages die. The kids are really hard. Unfortunately, my health insurance has crappy mental health coverage so I just have to get over it. From seeing overdoses at work, I would guess that drug use is about 50/50 males vs. females. So why are more men locked up?

The worst overdose lately was a male in his mid twenties that was found by his mom, in the basement on his knees head up against the wall, face purple and mouth covered in foam, a heroin set up by his side. The police officer called to the scene told me how heroin users shoot up. The police officer was not much older then the guy that died. The image follows me still and I never had to see him. Out of all the things in the world that man could have chosen to do that day, how was heroin the best option? Smart enough to prop himself up so he wouldn't die, but he did die anyway. All with a little white square, a spoon, a lighter, some cotton and a syringe. What a horrible, common waste.

In case you still think that we don't need more men raising kids:

From childhelp.org 1/31/2015 "Children are suffering from a hidden

epidemic of child abuse and neglect. Every year more than 3 million

reports of child abuse are made in the United States involving more

then 6 million children (a report can contain multiple children). The

United States has one of the worst records of industrialized nations -

losing an average between four and seven children every day to child

abuse and neglect. A report of child abuse is made every 10

seconds."

Physical and sexual abuse makes up most of the reports in a study by

CDK/Kaiser Permanete Adverse Childhood Experience Study. Do

we need more parents to step in? Yes. Are women trying to do it

alone probably worn out and poor? Yes. Who is doing the abusing

though?

Same website: "For new cases in 2008 alone, lifetime estimates of
lost worker productivity, health care costs, special education costs,
child welfare expenditures and criminal justice expenditures added up
to $124 billion. We must learn to recognize early signs of abuse in
order to save the 5 children that die every day from child abuse and
neglect. In 2012, state agencies identified an estimated 1,640 children
who died as a result of abuse and neglect - between four and five
children a day. However, studies also indicate significant
undercounting of child maltreatment fatalities by state agencies by
50% or more. More then 70% of the children who died as a result of
child abuse or neglect were two years of age or under. Around 80%

of child maltreatment fatalities involved at least one parent as a perpetrator." www.safehorizon.org "of the 2012 child abuse cases, 45.3% of the perpetrators were male and 53.5% were female." I read that to say that both males and females are endangering their own children.   Shouldn't   we   find   out   why?

5 Hurry! Big Chocolate Dick Special this Friday! Stop in For Half-off Tuesdays! Wednesday lunch Weiner and Wine Specials! Sign up for our Quickie Dickey Special Discount Frequent Fucker Program(TM).

The United States has the highest rate of incarceration of and developed country in the world. This is primarily a male issue. It is insanely expensive for our population if you add up court costs, wages lost, supporting prisoners, supporting prisoners children, etc. I don't think you have to think about it very long before you realize that most of these costs are not benefitting taxpayers in any way. We are, in fact, funding the whole enchilada. Is putting a drug user (over half the prison population) in jail really keeping anyone safer? Ever? The next user steps in within minutes I'm sure so it's no loss to the dealers we should be going after. I think the prison system and the

courts need to be brought back into a position where they are

following the will of the populace that they supposedly serve. I hope

that people smarter then me can figure out how to at least move in

that direction. If we made a five percent change in the right direction

every year, the impact on our economy would be tremendous. The

potential benefit to our children seems a given. Or we can make all

drugs legal so that we can make them safe.

Populations in prisons are growing dramatically. There has been a

ten-fold increase since 1980. So now the costs per prisoner are (on

average) $21,000 per year for minimum security, $25,378 low security,

$26,247 medium security and $33,930 for high security. Say an

average of $25,838 whereas probation costs $3,433 per offender.

The Federal budget for fiscal year 2013 is $6.9 billion - that's up 4%

over 2012. Drug offenses represent almost half of that cost. The

smallest percentage of the drug total is from pot so legalizing pot is

not going to help our prison costs to any large degree. Most of the

drug related prisoners are in for crack, meth and powder cocaine. So

crimes of every kind are down over the last ten years but prison populations grow? I think there is some dishonesty going on if we are going broke supporting people that don't pose a threat to society.

Where are we on alcohol and drug abuse in a nutshell? List of most abusive states, Business Insider, "In the course of reporting a story this morning on the fittingly high rate of alcohol dependence in Washington D.C.- the highest rate of any city in the country-we came across an interesting piece of information from the same study: Alaska, supposedly one of the most conservative states in the country, is also the state with the highest percentage of regular marijuana users." The state with the highest percentage of resident's age 12 or older that used cocaine in the last year: Rhode Island (3.87%). Not quite what you thought? No wonder nothing gets done in Washington, they are all stoned. I bet the lobbyists are sober. Can we please drug test all of our legislators? Let's give them a pay cut for each positive test and make them go to the VA hospital for their entire healthcare. There is no reason they shouldn't use the same and often the only healthcare available to our veterans who have so bravely lain there lives on the line. I will not even bring up the 175,000 homeless vets. Hey, I know, let's stop locking up innocent black men and turn the prisons into condos.

America's Prison Population Mar. 13,2014 by J.F./Minneapolis
"Who, What, Where, When and Why yesterday the Prison Policy
Initiative (PPI), a criminal justice research and advocacy group
released a report and chart that draws on various data sources to
present a fuller picture of precisely who is behind bars, and for what
reason. US has roughly 2.4m people locked up, with most of these
(1.36m) in state prisons." "The number of Federal laws has risen
from 3,000 in the early 1980s to over 4,450 by 2008. Many of these
have poor intent requirements, meaning people are being locked up
not to keep the rest of society safe but for technical violations of laws
they may not have known existed. This over reliance on
imprisonment can be seen most starkly, and sadly, by looking at the
juvenile population, which is just under 71,000 nationally. Around
11,600 are imprisoned for 'technical violations' of their probation or
parole terms, rather then because they committed a new crime.
Around 3,000 are locked up for things that aren't crimes for adults,
such as running away, truancy and incorrigibility." If they took my
kid away for being a kid I would raise holy hell. "There are almost

15,000 children behind bars whose most serious offense wasn't a crime. A separate 34,000 are technically not in the criminal justice system but rather are held by US Immigration and Customs Enforcement ICE.

There is a great graphic at www.truth-out.org called "Prison Inc." It's sweet check it out.

"Three companies receive the bulk of the prison contracts in the US: Corrections Corp of America, The GEO Group, and Management and Training Corp. Private prisons now house about half the country's prisoners, up from only about 10% a decade ago. The money these companies have spent on lobbying and campaign donations is estimated to be at least $45 million over the last decade, the AP found. The result has been hundreds of millions of dollars in yearly profits." So I think it's clear that they make more money from harsher and longer sentences. "Http//think progress.org/justice In Pennsylvania a judge has been given 17 years in prison for sentencing juveniles to a private facility in a 'cash for kids' scandal. Many of those sent to private facilities were locked up for minor offenses not normally subject to incarceration."

CBS News - The cost of a nation of incarceration - crime rate is actually down 40% over the last twenty years and the US is five percent of the world population but 25 percent of the world prisoners, as of 2012. This is mainly a male problem. I couldn't find any evidence that this great CBS story accomplished any change. What will it take when our media has no effect?

From MotherJones.com "We are living in boom times for the private prison industry. The Corrections Corporation of America (CCA), the nations largest owner of private prisons, has seen its revenue climb by more then 500 percent over the last two decades.... Last year the company made an offer to 48 governors to buy and operate their state-funded prisons. But what made CCA's pitch to those governors so audacious and shocking was that it included a so-called occupancy requirement, a clause demanding the state keep those newly privatized prisons at least 90 percent full at all times, regardless of weather crime was rising or falling." Some make deals for 100 percent occupancy. Can you imagine a guaranteed profit for your business?

literally no matter what happens, you get a big pile of money. There is no incentive to do anything but sit back and collect taxpayer money. Is this plan really serving us?

From Truth-Out.org's website: "According to the Left Business Observer, 'the Federal prison industry produces 100 percent of all military helmets, ammunition belts, bullet-proof vests, ID tags, shirts, pants, tents, bags, and canteens. Along with war supplies, prison workers supply 98 percent of the entire market for equipment assembly services; 93 percent of paints and paintbrushes; 92 percent of stove assembly; 46 percent of body armor; 36 percent of home appliances; 30 percent of headphones/microphones/speakers; and 21 percent of office furniture. Airplane parts, medical supplies, and much more: prisoners are even raising Seeing Eye dogs for blind people." Do the prisons pay any of these profits back to taxpayers? What kind of morons made these "deals"? They should be fired and fined.

Cost of prisons is somewhere between $31,286 to $60,000 per year, per inmate depending on the level of their incarceration. That number does not include the costs of the families they leave behind. One in thirty two adults, there are 2.4 million people in jail and 5 million on parole. This info is from the National Center for Victims of Crime. One in 5 girls and one in twenty boys is a victim of child sexual abuse. Perpetuators are overwhelmingly male and range from adolescent to elderly. Sixty percent of the time it is someone the child knows. How can we do better on keeping children away from molesters? The molesters are feeding the general mistrust of men being responsible for children. Are all men molesters? How do we change this perception? What makes a good man? Remember that criminals are successful mainly because they don't look like criminals. How many African-American families would at least have a fighting chance if their men were not in prison?

PPI Prison Policy Initiative, Federal prisons are only 10% of the people behind bars in the US and that includes immigration. Alabama and Louisiana have consistently maintained above average rates of incarceration, and their use of prison continues to grow. "The South consistently had a higher rate of incarceration then the other regions of the United States."

www.thinkprogress.org The United States has the largest population in the world - and it's growing, by Nichole Flatow Sept.18, 2014 "both in raw numbers and by percentage of the population, the United States has the most prisoners of any developed country in the world - and it has the largest prison population of any nation."

Is there any type of victim that ever actually received restitution? Even a fair shake in court is rare for most victims. Lawyers make lots of money but never go through anything. They tailor the system exactly to their benefit. So the system needs some work to truly serve the general population. It currently serves lawyers and prison owners. To the tune of 55 Billion yearly for Federal prisons alone.

They are doing something ... From the same Mother Jones article, "At the same time, private prison companies have supported and helped write 'three-strike' and 'truth-in-sentencing' laws that drive up prison populations". How the hell do so many boys end up in jail? Where are we going wrong? Where are we not going wrong with education is a better question. When both parents work, who raises the children? What if, as a parent, you actually want to love the little critters? Someone has to do it or we get the crazy mess we have now. I was a latchkey kid before we had a term for it. I lost my key all the time, so I was constantly breaking into my own house. It was not ok that no one knew where I was most of the time. I guess we don't care much if kids go missing these days (Parent People Problems ...am I right?). Where I live now, the high school kids are home by 2:30 in the afternoon. How are the parents supposed to supervise them? It's ridiculous. It is highly unsafe for everyone involved and (huge surprise) my local school is tops in heroin deaths. School should be from 9 to 5 year round - or whenever parents need to go to work for as long as that is the only way to pay for things. They do not need the summer off to work on the farm. They don't need three different start and three different end times for school, plus kindergarten. They are driving on icy roads to each bus stop where I live eight times a day. I can't think of a way to make it more expensive or more inconvenient for parents. Whose needs are being met by this schedule?

Can we take a step back and focus on the bigger issues? Start fresh with just a bunch of kids that need to learn to be people. Bonus points if these people can support themselves. What are our goals?

Do we want to produce self-supporting taxpayers so that they are

invested in the success of our country? Can we stop being

consumers that will blindly buy anything, even if it destroys their

health? Can number one in setting up the system be fucking safety?

We should be embarrassed that we let the current mess happen. Step

2 what are the things they need to know to accomplish our goals?

What is required of all the players involved? Blah, I can't solve it here

so I am just trying to start trouble. Letting the players in the game

know what is expected of them would go a long way towards the

success of this plan. What do we want from education?

I think prison should be absolutely horrible so that no one ever wants

to go back. You should loose something when you are found guilty

of a crime, something big. What about bringing back the stocks?

Embarrassment is very powerful. We can do it the way they did in

olden times...as far as I can tell...you place the person in the stocks

with a board with their crime that they were found guilty of spelled

out. Exactly what they did next to their face. This happens in the

busiest part of the town where they completed their offense. You then provide a basket of not new fruit or veg (something gross) and maybe a basket of rocks depending on their crime. Let someone hang out and mess him or herself for a day and I think they will think twice about being a horrible person. Can we do this for rape? I know some chicks that want to throw some rocks and have a talk with their attackers. People would at least get a chance to tell these losers what we think of them. Put in a camera and a web feed with people who will throw rotten tomatoes at the target of your choice for a buck, processed from your phone. Come on PayPal you split off from eBay. Live a little! They would then send you the feed from your rotten tomato (or rock), which you now own to do with as you please. There is money to be made off of actual bad guys for taxpayers! Let's call it the Splatter the Scum network! Do your friends and family love you enough to sit with you and defend you? Will they change your pants when you mess yourself (360 no scope butt cam!)? How have we gone from the stocks and embarrassment to pen pal programs? I think embarrassment is very powerful! They go hurt people or steal things and we give them a place to live and privacy? We are clearly sending the wrong message when prisoners are treated better then workers in China (from what I've heard).

Can we do the same with prisons and schools? You have no system. The problem you need to solve is bad people hurting good people. Good people get together and decide they are willing to pay to keep the bad people away from them. Ok, now set up a system for accomplishing the goal of keeping people safe. Do we also want to pay to keep their property safe? Probably, ok so add that on to the rules. We are not accomplishing these two things right now. You can sit and debate all day whether it is worse to live with jerks that might beat you up or (taking your physical health) or quietly steal all of your retirement money so that you are forced to work until you breathe your last breath. The fact remains that we are being bankrupted as a nation by a system that is not even meeting these two goals. It's not always clear who is bad and who is good. So what we need are some smart people looking out for the interests of people busy working for taxable wages. We are sure paying, we're just not getting.

There are two crimes that women commit more then men: prostitution and running away as juveniles. "The average incarcerated father has 2.1 children. Forty-two percent of state prisoners reported living with one or more of their minor children in the period immediately prior to their incarceration." (Glaze & Maruschak, 2008). Is there any way to get the prisoners to help with the kids? Can they grow them food? If they have limited money, they may be solely eating off the dollar menus at fast food places. The only winners in the current system are private prisons and their shareholders.

If woman suddenly started committing half as many crimes as men, the costs would topple our economy. Why do men get to do all the crime? I guess women don't have as much free time to commit crimes. Mostly because we all have second jobs keeping the house together, cleaning, cooking and raising 70 percent of the next generation of kids in the U.S. (I made that up, I can't find data on how many kids are raised by women only or by extension single parents.)

"According to the Bureau of Justice statistics, in 2007 an estimated 744,200 state and federal prisoners in the United States were fathers to 1,599,200 children under the age of 18."(Glaze and Meruschak, 2008). I'm not what you would call a fan of private prisons because the money factor fundamentally works against our goals of having less crime.

"Six Shocking Revelations About how Private Prisons Make Their Money - by www.alternet.org [These contracts run] counter to many states' public policy goals of reducing the prison population and increasing efforts for inmate rehabilitation' the report states 'When policymakers received the 2012 CCA letter, some worried the terms of CCA's offer would encourage criminal justice officials to seek harsher sentences to maintain the occupancy rates required by contract. Policy decisions should be based on creating and maintaining a criminal justice system that protects the public interest, not ensuring corporate profits." "September 20, 2013 imagine living in a country where prisons are private corporations that profit from keeping their beds stocked at, or near, capacity and the governing officials scramble to keep contractual lockup quotas". Imagine that taxpayers would have to pay for any empty beds should crime rates fall below that quota. Surprise! You already live there."

With the article there is a great graphic that shows a dude with a bar code on his forehead. www.americanhumanist.org "The cost to house a prisoner being held by US Immigrations and Customs Enforcement has risen from $80 per person, per day to $166 today, with the government refusing to provide details explaining the difference."

"In addition to investors in private prisons pushing for their increased use to increase revenues, prison guard unions are lobbying (www.caprogressivemessage.com/2011) to stop reforms that would allow for more early release eligibility and shorter sentences. If there are fewer prisoners, there is a reduced need for guards which reduces the size and strength of the unions, providing a motivation to work against any move to reduce the number of those behind bars." I don't know if this statement is fair. I know of many people who work in prisons that have criminal justice degrees and advanced training that are waiting for the opportunity to serve as police officers.

The math is close to screwing us all over...Total population in 2010 -

308,745,538 with 194,296,087 to pay taxes and take care of

114,449,451 people. We haven't got the extra money for prison

corruption.

Here are more stats from the U.S. Census ...because I am having

trouble moving on.

Table 314 "Forcible Rape" "Forcible Rape as defined in the FBIs

Uniform Crime Reporting (UCR) Program, is the carnal knowledge

of a female forcibly against her will."

1990 to 2009, 1990 - 102,560 in 2009 the total was 81,280 so rape

crime is down despite population growth. Why this steady drop in

this time period? Can we keep up whatever good work happened?

Can we celebrate? How many women and men have better lives? I

guess it's harder to notice when something slowly goes away. What

happened? The private prisons want to keep us scared so we keep

paying them to house their own free labor. Have they thought about

pimping these guys out? They are just sleeping at night after all!

They could be earning triple money off these dudes, not just double.

Chocolate specials for bored housewives on cellblock 6...after school drop off special get yours before you do your chores!

In looking at numbers for child abuse and neglect, I never realized it was 50/50 male and female victims. I would have thought it was more girls then boys. I don't know why. It is a tiny bit more girls then boys but not significant. I guess I was holding a prejudice against men without even realizing it. How many more things do I assume to be true that are completely wrong? Scary how easily you can just let yourself believe something about a group of people without even questioning it. I guess I'm mentally lazy but I want to change my ways. Accurate news would really help.

How about publish real crime and imprisonment stats monthly broken down by sex and race so that we can see what is going on. We sure pay enough to get real-time data. Hey can there be an accurate crime application? We should know how many prison beds we currently have filled vs. empty and what out prisoners are doing with their time. We are buying after all. We all work for the freedom to choose how we spend our time and whom we spend our time with. So who's costing us the most?

In trying to find information about who is committing most crimes and where I am finding it's very hard to get coherent info. Ah, but we do know who's getting hurt. US <u>Census</u> stats: total cases of abuse and neglect 2009 United States population under 1875,512,062. Reports 2,000,488. Children subject to investigation: 3,635,688, victims: 762,940. Table 312 Cheerily titled: "Homicide Trends 1980 to 2008" Total victims in 1980 was 23,040 (17,803 male, 5,237 female). In 2008 Total victims 16,272 (12,731 male and 3,541 female). So prison populations are up but murder is way down? Why is it so difficult to get accurate information? Someone, somewhere, probably that taxpayers pay, fucking knows.

CCA (biggest private prison management company in the US) website:
"Taxpayer savings. In a peer reviewed study published by the Independent Institute and supported by the private corrections industry, economists found that partnership corrections generates from 12% to 58% in long-run taxpayer savings, giving states more money to invest in additional public safety and recidivism-reducing

programs." They think we are too stupid to pay attention. This has worked perfectly so far. How do we get always from those entities devoted to keeping us in the dark but making us feel like we are in the light?

Donors Trust has been described by Mother Jones as "the dark-money ATM of the conservative movement. Why do we care? Because DonorsTrust funds 95% of the Franklin Center for Government Integrity has strong ties to The Independence Institute. Simple. Did you know we even had a center for government integrity? Does PITA own a butcher house? It must be underfunded.

The reason we need to watch for things like Donors Trust is that they quietly fund things like the American Legislative Exchange Council (ALEC), a mechanism for corporate interests to help write state laws. Translation: the bribes to states for acting right have to go through something that sounds legit. We need some super bean counters to get on this shit.

God forbid any of us should be able to actually read our laws and make sense of them. I may not be a smart man but where there is subterfuge, there is a reason and an outstretched hand wanting my money. There have been cries for so many years to our own government to "Show us the money" that most people have lost hope of figuring out how it all works. We just keep our heads down and work. I don't know about you but I'm tired.

I need to put all of this corruption aside because I'm getting distracted but I would be on board with a video game where you get to shoot down lobbyists! At least be a little sneakier with the corruption please. My Dad told me that you loose all your rights when you go to prison. I didn't realize taxpayers would lose their rights when they send someone to prison.

DrugWarfacts.org: "Marijuana essentially became illegal in 1937 pursuant to the Marijuana Tax Act. The use of marijuana required the payment of a tax for usage; failure to pay the tax resulted in a large fine or stiff prison time for tax evasion. Harry J. Anslinger, the first commissioner of the Federal Bureau of Narcotics, efforts to eradicate marijuana at the state level. States followed and by 1952

nearly all states had anti-narcotics laws in place." So because of one

douche trying to make a job for himself, it has cost people millions of

dollars and lives lost to fight a drug that has never killed anyone. Yes

for realsies. So we in the US have to import something we could

grow perfectly well.

I keep coming back to those people that may support me in my old

age. I think it's a no brainier that children raised without two parents

are more likely to end up in trouble because economic problems in

the household are a given. I know there are many stories of moms

receiving huge money for raising their kids and spending it all on

themselves. After 12 years in the court system, I've seen every

person I have met along the way dealing with no money to take care

of his or her children through non-payment by the non-custodial

parent. Many times we know they have income but can't prove the

paper trail. The end result is always the same: the custodial parent

(the person taking care of the child everyday) goes into personal debt

and has no retirement to raise their child. There are millions just like

me putting their child first. I will have to work until I'm dead at this rate. It just takes a lot of money to have a roof over their heads etc. Why can't I do better? All I could afford was a foreclosed home. I worked really hard on the house and learned a lot (thank you YouTube!) but still, the maintenance costs of an older house are killing me. I'm lucky I got a house at the right time.

If the one parent that is raising the child has to earn the money for all that, the kids are left to raise themselves. The best a parent can do is try to work while they are in school. That is not as easy as it sounds. What if the child is sick? Needs to get to the dentist, doctor, etc.? Now, that one parent is missing work too much so their employer may say but bye. What about taking care of the house? We are not living in the best places and something seems to always need repair. This can add to the economic burden. If that one person gets sick, the whole thing falls apart. Right now, God help me if the furnace breaks! I am too old for prostitution!

Male dependence on the prison system is expensive: For all different types of crime that police enforce, 75 to 80 percent of offenders are male. "CCA Charles L. Overby, Director CCA, former Pulitzer prize winning editor. American Correctional Association (ACA) CCA incorporated in 1983 - rated one of the top 50 military friendly employers. Jan 2013 celebrated 30 years of success and reorganized into a REIT (Real Estate Investment Trust). Definition per Wikipedia "A company that owns, and in most cases, operates income-producing real estate. On investopedia.com: A security that sells like a stock on the major exchanges and invests in real estate directly either through properties or mortgages. REITs receive special tax considerations and typically offer investors high yields as well as a highly liquid method of investing in real estate."

Thomas Sowell: "In American criminal trials, for example, before a murderer is sentenced, the law permits his unhappy childhood to be taken into account. Seldom is there any claim that the person who was murdered had anything to do with that presumptively unhappy childhood. In a notorious 1996 case in California, the victim was a 12 year-old girl. Who had not even been born when the murderer was supposedly going through his unhappy childhood? It is only from a cosmic perspective that his childhood had any bearing on the crime."

This stupid crap has to stop. Our court systems are crowded and expensive. Many rape cases go uninvestigated for years and we are wasting time on hearing about events that have no bearing on anything. We don't hear about the victim's past or the effect on the family of the victim. Can we please stick to only what the case is about? I was raped - should I just go kill some men? Does my prior bad luck make it ok for me to do anything I want? Hmmm I think I will target sexual predators oohhh!! There is a handy listing with their address on it. How convenient! I had only considered this online list in terms of protecting my daughter from weirdoes. Just kidding, I'm a single-mom; I don't have time for crime (except perhaps trying to write this book, I never got the best grades in English). The sex-offender registry has been hijacked by bureaucracy how can we return it to a useful tool for knowing where the real sickos are? We paid for a system to keep us safe and now it's meaningless. Hmmm I'm starting to see a theme. I can be so slow!

"Through no fault of their own" has become epidemic in the US. If none of us are responsible for our circumstances or actions, then none of us are responsible for our achievements either. You can't have it both ways. I work for a Catholic Hospital chain that, for the twelve years that I have worked there, does not consider Good Friday or Easter holidays, and as such, does not pay holiday pay to workers required to work these days. I hate that every Easter I miss spending twelve hours of it with my daughter and don't even get holiday pay at a Catholic hospital. They have a special exemption that also means that they also don't have to pay for birth control because they don't believe in it. I wish I were making this up. Yes, they even made it through the last round of the federal government trying to make them cover it with an exception in 2015. So let me get this straight, you can have a bunch of kids, you just can't see them or have any paid time off to have with them. More and more people are refusing to do it. Most of the people working at hospitals that get hourly pay are female with advanced degrees and training. We are also exposed to disease, dying and moving fat people all the time that can't move themselves. When was the last time you saw a kid die? I bet never for the accountants that run hospitals.

95 percent of violence and killing is attributable to men. Um that

means that only men can fix it. They have been in power for some time and things are still messed up and corruption is rampant. Would actually paying police officers help? They need to get paid or they will be corrupted. I think we can call it and say we have had enough of the current mess. None of the stuff we are doing now is working. Can we look at examples from less-corrupt places that may have programs that work? How about if police just keep our bodies and our money safe? No prostitution, no drugs.... completely new training for domestic violence. You get locked in a cell together with a therapist and a bouncer until you figure your shit out.

6 THE QUIET ANGER EATING MEN

What is the worst thing you can do to a man? I really don't know.

Why the hell don't I know? Many horrible things happen to women.

Here's a story you didn't ask for:

I went to a Hawaiian party at the house of some friends. I had been

to parties there plenty of times. I remember the punch of the night

was blue. I don't remember who brought me a red solo cup full but I

never finished the drink. Imagine: you wake up disoriented and

naked on a bedroom floor (not yours) all you can see is under a bed

because your head is turned that way and you can't move any muscles

in your body, not even your head. All of your effort goes into

breathing. Were you not breathing? Hard to tell. You fight for

breath. Then you wake up naked on a bedroom floor and it's really hard to breathe because someone is crushing you under their naked body. I can't look at them. I can't move my head from my current view of under a bed. I can't feel anything except that it is hard to breathe. Then I wake up someplace and there is yelling because now I can feel my legs and I am holding them closed with all the strength I'm not using to breathe. Then I wake up under a pile of coats and it's hard to breathe so I roll over onto my side. Then I wake up on a bed under the covers at my friend's house (all dudes I have hung out with before). I am confused. I searched the house for my purse and clothes, which were all over the place. They said that I got drunk and was dancing on the table and passed out. I had part of one drink they made for me while we were waiting for the party to start. I guess I was the party. My friends had been sent away with a story that I left with some guy. Damn, I had just gotten over being raped sober in the middle of the afternoon by my "boyfriend" of three months in front of a group of about 10 people. How come men can get drunk and not get raped? It's not fair to always have a vagina with me. What if I just want to go be a person? Should we all have custom digital chastity belts to keep our vagina safe?

I have always worked on the assumption that I'm average looking.

Does all this extra attention and rapes mean I'm pretty? Does it just mean that I look like an easy target? I clearly did a suck ass job of raising myself.

I cried a lot. My shame at having no idea what happened with my body for a long period of time kept me from talking to anybody. I had no idea who to accuse, I went back and tried to ask the guys that were my "friends" what the hell had gone on and they told me that I was an obnoxious drunk. I didn't hear about the existence of date rape drugs until years later. I assumed it was all my fault. I asked my friends that were supposed to meet me at the party why they just left me there. They had been told that a guy that I really liked had whisked me off to a romantic dinner at a nice restaurant. They thought that I was a bitch for not even telling them goodbye.

I went back to the health center and they bought the exact same story and didn't ask any questions. I was lucky I only got crabs. Now there is a great sentence.

I got busy walling off another little section of myself to keep it separate from my actual life. If I don't face what happened then I don't get the gift or lesson that the experience holds for me. No one died, no life was created, I didn't get AIDS, I am less naive and desperate men will do anything.

I wonder what the total number of men is that have done all this raping? Are they all married to mean wives that torture them every day and that torture secretly makes them feel better about all their raping that they did in college. If these rapists walled their actions off like I did then, is it slowly chewing at them from the inside as they watch their daughters play and grow. The guilt piling up as they fully realize the brutality of their actions?

I wonder about the demographics of rapists. Mine were pretty good looking so I can't believe they couldn't get sex. What exactly were they going for? Fun? Relief of social pressure? Was it a dare? I'm sorry they had to do what they did. I no longer take responsibility for their actions.

Relationship of victim to rapist from the US Bureau of Labor Statistics: current or former intimate partner 26%, another relative 7%, friend or acquaintance 38%, stranger 26%. So 1.3 women 18 years and older are raped each minute.

More recent data from the Bureau of Labor Statistics: 2013 report rape in the U.S. 28.6% and Canada 1.5%. Something is messed up

there. Are 28.6% of American women raped? We live right next

door! In Canada females can go topless in public and personal pot is

legal. Let's try their plan! It's weird that the pay gap and the amount

of rape are about the same percentage.

Men select women and treat women exactly the same as they treat

their cars. Think about it. I realized this was a thing when I rented a

basement room from a guy with two cars: a work truck and a nice car

for showing off. He was unable to say which one he liked better and

had the same dilemma deciding what type of woman he wanted to

share his life with. He liked hanging out with smart and sassy women

but felt that a perfect looking one should only arouse him. So he

bounces back and forth not knowing what he wants. With men who

treat their cars like crap you will find that they don't take care of you

either. The other side is equally as scary, the perfectly detailed car is

creepy because no one is that perfect all the time. Human female

bodies fart; burp and periods can be messy.

What kind of car do I represent to men? Here is a list that I made trying to figure it out: Ferrari - temperamental and expensive but really beautiful, Mercedes - nice curves, expensive maintenance, nice truck - like a nurse expensive but useful and dependable, Honda Civic - will last forever if you treat it right and useful but not too flashy, Beater Truck - no maintenance, could break at any time but it's paid off and you don't have to worry about taking care of it, Creeper Van - not dependable, still technically a vehicle, you don't want anyone to see you in it.

What do women have to do to be considered human? Medical science won't even look at our periods! How we ever tackle that silent killer uterine cancer? Why do we give things a female pronoun? I am not a fucking boat, car, ship...I am far more...I am a chick! Stop being assholes! A boat or a car or a plane is an IT! Not a SHE! I know that the English language is generally. A female strength but if you are going to earn 30 percent more money, you can fucking earn it.

Speaking about social and sexual inequality...Thomas Sowell, "The

Quest for Cosmic Justice."

"Nor should we imagine that quantifiable economic differences or political and social inequalities exhaust the disabilities of the less fortunate. Affluent professional people have access to all sorts of free knowledge and advice from highly educated and knowledgeable friends and relatives, perhaps substantial financial aid in time of crisis from some of these same sources. They also tend to have greater access to those with political power, whether through direct contacts or through the simple fact of being able to make an articulate presentation in terms acceptable to political elites. Moreover, The fact that the affluent tend to have the air of knowledgeable people makes them less likely to become targets for many of the swindlers who prey on the ignorant and the poor."

We are not far, if any distance at all from men having all the power. There are many types of power that women are yet to taste, let alone share. Women generally pay more for every single thing they need then men do.

More by Sowell. "Even in legitimate businesses, 'the poor pay more', as the title of a book said some years ago because it costs more to deliver goods and services to low-income, high-crime neighborhoods, where insurance and other costs are higher. In short, statistical inequalities do not begin to exhaust the advantages of the advantaged or the disadvantages of the disadvantaged." It also creates a problem that children believe that they will turn into people just like those around them. I accomplish so many things that are good in the name of setting a good example for my daughter. Way more then I would do just for me. How can women have equality of paying for goods and services? Car repair? Home repairs? I'm tired of feeling second class.

Sowell then goes on to say that what we call "social justice" is actually "anti-social justice" because it disregards the costs to the rest of society. Like a program that unfairly awards hiring only men because health insurance costs for young men are generally lower then for females having children. This is in contrast to the large and ever growing "taking class" of humans that live off the work of others. Why do I need to pay for someone else because they didn't take care of themselves? Why am I responsible when they have a baby with a problem? They usually have insurance. Stupidity pays pretty well these days. Hundreds of X-rays later now note that I am not a doctor, but your knees and your back hurt because you are fat. Nothing else can fix it but taking off some fat. I have never force fed anyone, why do I have to pay? I'm supposed to live on a budget and can't take into account the child support that I am supposed to get but there is no filter on Federal programs for support?

I'm not thin myself, I know it sucks but that's it. I think "Atlas Shrugged" by Ayn Rand should be required reading! A favorite quote from that book "I swear by my life and my love of it that I will never live for the sake of another man, nor ask another man to live for mine." I can't resist one from The Fountainhead by the same author: "Don't help me or service me but let me see it once, because I need it. Don't work for my happiness. Show me yours - show me that it is possible - show me your achievement - and the knowledge will give me courage for mine." We should take our kids to work once a month at least. We actively separate them from economic reality then we are surprised when they treat us like ATMs.

I read that when women cry, men feel squeezed, like they have to get away. I have been trying to understand this. Is it because they don't know how to fix it? (A hug) Is it because they don't allow themselves

the luxury of tears? (Not fair) they feel like tears are a weapon being

used against them? (This is wrong) My response to another person's

tears is to hug them and listen to them. One of the two will usually

help them see the big picture and the world in a better light. I don't

think that I can fix anyone's problems but possibly my own.

I am still having trouble with Jack. The Way of Men by Jack

Donovan captures the "silent, stifling rage of men everywhere who

find themselves at odds with the over-regulated, over-civilized,

politically correct modern world." I don't really know what he means

by over-civilized. Because we shower? Expect that you will NOT

pull women around by their hair? Most men I know absolutely love

electronics. Is this being over-civilized? Can I please get a pedophile

warning on the GPS on my phone? Can we please microchip these

fuckers?

Not helping

Husband bashing...I don't understand it. You are telling everyone

but the person that can change the situation. Frankly, I can't listen to it anymore. If you are that unhappy - move, change, and get off your ass. The most common reason I get back when I say this is that they don't have the money. Poverty, saving one marriage at a time! What an unknown superhero! Prostituting yourself and being a wife sound a lot the same to me. I don't want to feel handcuffed by money or a man.

Weird Sex Thoughts

Let's look at sex as a basic need. Let's talk in terms of a sandwich to simplify things. I enter into an agreement with you that says that I will only get my sandwiches from you because I trust that they are the best, healthiest, non-GMO, pesticide-free organic sandwiches on Earth. You enter into this agreement because I am the only one that wants your sandwiches. Suddenly, everyone wants your sandwiches. What do you do? I never want to someone to stay in an agreement with me because I am they only one that once wanted their sandwiches. In a system where sandwich deals are supposed to be exclusive but there are no parameters for meeting each other's needs there is bound to be a mismatch between needs at some point. It seems set up for failure.

I can accept that I may be too stupid to understand marriage. I never want someone to "love" me because I am the only sandwich that is available. Each time I was asked I politely said no thank you and returned any jewelry that was offered in exchange for exclusive sandwich rights. Bondage jewelry is how I see it. Have you heard of the Tiffany bracelets that the man literally locks on his woman and she can't get it off without his key? No fucking thanks!

Why do chicks get a big engagement rock? It's a down payment on the fact that you are doing all the work from here on out. Not a bad deal for the dude. Payments on a ring in exchange for a clean house, meals, sex, raising children and most of the time a second income. What are women getting? How can I think of love when I'm tired from doing everything? It's taking advantage and its shitty.

Why are you looking for tools to use against each other? Sex is not a tool a vacuum is a tool.

<u>Treating men like they are not humans with emotions.</u> Everyone

needs to learn emotional intelligence to have the best possible life but

it's not something I've ever seen on a curriculum other then in

Psychology classes (yes, I really have a Bachelor degree in

Psychology, with a Chemistry minor if you care). Even then it wasn't

presented in a practical and useful manner. I don't see how schools

can't slip that in along with a bit of money management? I know I've

had to learn both the hard way. That just seems ridiculous. I want

girls to learn to code as much as the next person but let's teach some

basics too. Heck, I want to go learn to code, maybe I'm too old. If

you already hate me by now-don't worry, I don't think I will ever

write another book. I'm exhausted, I ramble and my brain is very

unruly. I will stick some of my unrelated theories in an appendix for

your entertainment.

<u>Men's inability to rationally negotiate their needs</u>

A final personal story that, I hope, will show why these issues are

important:

"I can't live with you or without" you was the song he sang to me,

and then he raped me in front of our friends. wtf? We were just

sitting there watching a game on TV in the afternoon not even drinking.

Half time started and the room went silent, everyone was waiting for something.

My boyfriend stood up and reached out his hand to me. He led me into a bedroom off the living room, which was surprisingly clean. He said nothing but forced me down onto the bed. He didn't shut the door. The doorway filled up with faces: his roommates, their girlfriends and random people I didn't know. He didn't kiss me, didn't smile he ripped off my clothes and forced his six foot six self onto then into me. I was yelling for help and for him to stop. He was a player for the college baseball team and very strong. I didn't have a chance to change what was happening. I honestly don't think most men could have stopped him. I had so many feelings all at once that I was crying and hysterical. We had never had sex. We had kissed but that's all. He never pushed to have sex with me right up until he raped me. Luckily he finished quickly. It was only later I realized there was no condom.

When he was done, I grabbed my clothes and ran back to my apartment naked and crying. All I could think of was "thank God no one saw me". So clearly I was not making sense. None of my three roommates were home. I curled up in a corner cried and rocked for a while. At least I'm no stranger to self-soothing. I had to work at 6:30pm so I got in the shower and dressed for my waitressing job. It was nickel beer night. You get a 12 oz. plastic cup of beer for a nickel. It was crazy busy and college kids drink down to their last nickel, then leave. They are not the best tippers.

It was next-level weird to run serving people and fend off pinching fingers so soon after what happened. I vaguely wondered how I wouldn't punch the next guy that hit on me in the face.

Only females are stupid enough to work waitressing for $2.00 an hour in a college town. I was young, didn't have a car and I needed the money (rim shot).

Today I vaguely wonder how I worked until two in the morning, cleaned up and then walked home across a dark campus. Nothing ever happened to me walking on campus at night. It's the people you know that you have to watch out for.

He called and called me after that. He wanted to talk about our relationship. I spent time wondering how to forgive him. I went to the student health center to make sure that I was ok. They asked why

I wanted to be screened for diseases. I made up a story that my

boyfriend cheated on me. No one asked if anything was wrong when

tears streamed fresh down my face during the exam as I was vividly

reminded of what had happened to my vagina. How did they ignore

the obvious recent trauma? I looked it wasn't pretty. They just

rushed on with their day. I was used to being invisible. I was actively

working on being numb in every way. I was too successful. Luckily I

didn't catch anything and didn't get pregnant. I did all in secret. I

was too afraid and embarrassed to seek out help or confide in anyone

for fear they would reject me.

I finally agreed to go for a walk with my x-boyfriend. We walked a

long way in the daylight and in silence. He told me stuff that I

already knew about him: that his dad had left his mom with two

young sons to raise on her own and that he had to take care of his

little brother a lot. He resented and hated his father. I told him I

forgive him but that I never wanted to see him again. I'm not sure

how he thought things would work between us after what he did. He

got drafted to a professional baseball farm team whatever that means.

I never considered reporting him because at that time reporting an assault against an athlete was especially frowned upon and would have been another horrible ordeal for me to go through. I just couldn't face it. Since it was a plan that a group of people must have been in on, I had no faith that I would be heard. If I "won" he would lose his sports scholarship and what he was trying to do was make enough money to support his mom and little brother. I decided it was unlikely that he would rape again so who would I really be helping by pursuing it further? I never considered that inside I was shattered, my trust in men and humanity was broken and I was numb to any emotions. I guess I tried to mentally bubble wrap myself. I decided to take a year off from dating and turned to beer for support.

Denial is lonely and comfy. I took the fact that I didn't get pregnant as a confirmation that I chose the right path. Without a little reminder, I could just pretend that it never happened. I shoved all of the mess to the back of my brain for further evaluation at some undetermined future date.

A year later, I decided to reclaim my sex life.

I am trying to figure out how and why I put my needs and myself behind my rapists needs. What made me think his priorities were more important then mine? I guess it's because it never occurred to me that I wouldn't be ok. I drew strength from a mess. What traumatized me the most is that his roommates cheered for him while he was raping me. I was screaming for help. The girlfriends just watched. I still can't get my head around it.

Is it because I was a middle child in an alcoholic household that it never occurred to me that anyone would take care of me or help me through it? I still haven't told my siblings. I have this nice big sturdy wall now to keep me safe. I'm not sure what it will take for me to get rid of the wall. I guess when I feel strong enough I will just walk away from my wall.

I am starting to look at the whole thing with a thought that maybe the way that I handled it was the best way that I knew how and I am really strong. I do need to see that I didn't need to do it the way I did and maybe I could have reached out and let someone get close to me. Nah, that's crazy talk.

Why did I share this? For attention of course, also I don't want to protect the little bubble in my head by keeping it separate from the people that I love. If they don't love me anymore after hearing what happened then fuck them. I hope that me sharing my story may help someone else maybe think about their rape experience differently. A man that I know told me that if I write this book then no man will ever marry me. He should have said no loser. I don't want to grow old alone or with someone that I have to keep secrets from. It's not my fault men chose to rape me. It is my responsibility to figure out what I can learn from it. Can I use it to help others? When I just let these junky feelings stew and ferment inside of me, it only hurts me.

How many times do I need to be raped to feel pretty?

Yes I was screaming for help at the top of my lungs. I lost faith in humanity that day. I know that he was an otherwise sweet kid who grew up without a Dad and had to play Dad to his younger brother. His friends basically talked him into it but that is not an excuse. There is never a good enough excuse for doing that to a person.

Why can't Vikings just burn the village? Why rape the women too?

Don't these assholes have Moms, daughters or sisters? Why do

women have to be ground to bits for men to feel like men?

Few human acts more completely negate the human spirit then rape.

The most cowardly act against women is rape (or is it the police

departments for example Detroit the shoved 11,000 rape kits in their

basement and never examined them?) Rape is a clear indication that

a society is out of control. I know I need to quit talking about it.

Rape stats are down but we don't know why.

I do have one more question. Where did all these rapists wander off

to? Are they married with children? Who did they marry? Do they

owe the women they raped an apology? Any attempt at returning

their faith in humanity? Where are they now? What are rapist's

parents like? I mean is there a common type? I'm not sure we have

really thought this through. I'm not about blaming parents for

everything but it's men in their 20s, they are barely people.

So theoretically there are a bunch of men running around now that are my age who did terrible things to girls in school. What should they do with their sad little selves? I think they should be awesome dads that talk to their daughters and tell them how to avoid assholes like they were. If they never married perhaps they could roam the streets like quiet superheroes ruining the lives of pedophiles, and policing college campuses to keep women safe and make sure the crop of current pricks never get jobs out of school. How did these men make the decision that another person's life is just there for their entertainment? What would they think about being on the other end of that equation? Do they feel like they are already there so things can't get any worse?

I cannot get my head around the thought process that makes drugging and raping another human ok. What is it that they tell themselves as they plan: buying the drug, figuring out the dose? setting up the opportunity and location to take from someone something they would never give willingly? That's a long time to think about it. It's not just an impulse item at the grocery store like gum. Oh God, is it?

Is it really not just I? Nooooo...even today raping and pillaging are the norm. Rape stats: Rape, Abuse & Incest National Network (RAINN) "Approximately 2/3 of rapes were committed by someone known to the victim. 43% of rapes occur between 6:00 pm and midnight. 24% occur between midnight and 6:00 am. The average age of a rapist is 31 years old. 52% are white. 22% of imprisoned rapists report that they are married. In 1 in 3 sexual assaults, the perpetrator was intoxicated 30% with alcohol, 4% with drugs. Rapists are more likely to be a serial criminal then a serial rapist. 46% of rapists who were released from prison were re-arrested within 3 years of their release for another crime. Was the real crime in my situation that I was drugged etc. or that my first thought when realizing what happened was "why would they go through all that trouble to have sex with me?" If it was really that big of deal to them they might have asked me.

Maybe it's just a few rotten apples spoiling the bunch. Should we blame they way boys are socialized for the whole mess? "When men think they should keep their worries hidden, they stop talking to their wives about things that matter to them. That was leading to increased tension and distance between the partners." Why would

men have the idea that clamming up and not communicating would

protect their wives from something? When has not communicating

ever made something better? But it seems to me the go-to response

for men. Are they afraid of their anger? It makes us women feel

completely worthless when you clam up and go away. I think you

guys know that. The fact that everyone is responsible for their own

actions is often waived for men. They are so human as to not even

be responsible for what they do with their own body parts. Sound

super-human to me but I'm barely human with my vagina and all.

Responsibility is not a four-letter word. What do we do with the men

of quiet desperation that have committed no crimes? We need to

love them and not lump them in with the losers. How do we tell the

difference? Could they wear a hat or something? We are not

honoring the men who deserve it. We are not appropriately

punishing those who don't.

7 SUMMARY AND HAPPY ENDING

So it seems like many men are simply supporting their own

amusement rather then helping their own children. Here is an

example of some dudes that deserve respect:

Bloomberg BusinessWeek article called Dorks Win about a fantasy

sports leagues sometimes raking in $27,500 in entry fees per second.

"Revenue last year, after paying out $564.5M in winnings, was

$57.3M." At the end of the article one of the winners, Scott Hanson,

said, "I'd consider doing the whole stay-at-home dad slash daily

fantasy sports player thing." He is happily married and won over 2M.

Wow! Fantasy sports! Who knew? Even at the events where they

set up a pub-like atmosphere, they had some playboy bunnies walking

around that were basically ignored because it's more of a family thing.

I like that! Fan Duel is the company that was profiled by Bloomberg.

Sounds like a man's dream come trues thanks to technology! What else can we dream up that's fun and let's more people be parents to their kids?

Are games so good now that some men prefer them to their families? Gamers: www.technobuffalo.com "according to NPD, the most extreme game players make up eight percent of the 18,872 people it polled in January and those people earned that label by the fact that they play games an average of 48.5 hours a week and their average age is 42 years old! So add a job on top of their gaming and remembering that there are 168 hours in a week, they aren't being left time to do a whole lot of other things during their week. How do they sleep and hold down jobs? Now they have some serious time management skills! I don't think we need to take games away from men. I think there is an untapped multiplayer market in women playing together. May as well pull kids in too. Interact on some level! If women played even half as many games as men, what would happen? Would the economy crash? Would no one run the PTO? Would naked under fed children run wild in the streets? Would that really be so horrible? Oh yeah we'd have to kill all the pedophiles first. Can we just do that anyway? (Just the ones that hurt people,

not everyone who ever had a thought).

In a disturbing trend, if some men can't feel big by making women

feel small and helpless, then they don't want to play at all. I guess

they go off and say to themselves "I will just go love this motorcycle

or classic car or a boat - revenue of the recreational vehicle thanks

you to the tune of $18 billion, up 11.8 percent for 2013 according to

IBISWorld.com. Nowhere on their site can I find what IBIS stands

for. I want to engage these men and bring them out of their RV safe

bunkers and basements of all kinds and make sure they know we

need them. Can we somehow make it worth their while to come out

and play with us? Can we find out what made them quit caring if

that's what happened? The next generation really needs them. If

dads will not step up, then grandpa needs to if he can. I want to

bring these men back into participating in our lives. They have so

much knowledge and experience to offer. It is a horrible travesty

that it is being wasted on detailing vehicles. Dudes - tell us where

you want to be! Not sitting in a lazy boy all day. You had that and

you messed it up. Also it kills you.

What do we have to offer them in return? The love and respect they

deserve? Just taking care of yourself can be challenging for a male or

female. Taking on supporting a family should be held in the highest

respect - no matter who does it. How can we reward the things that

we actually value? Is the stuff that makes us feel good actually

incredibly boring? Everyone says what matters most at the end of

their life is people who love and care about them. How, as a society,

can we reward that instead of punishing it with unpaid leave for

parents, taking away insurance, having school for part of the year and

all different times of the day, making quality food expensive and hard

to find and punishing kids for being kids. We are making them to sit

and do low level secretarial work all day. What does that prepare

them for? Factory workers are no longer needed. We need thinkers

not drones.

What if we all have a funeral every ten years? Ok, that's silly but what

in the world can wake us up to see each other and live the priorities

that we profess to have? How can we get men to see that birth

control is their problem too? How stupid are they that they can't see

that the populations with the deluxe bodies that make people need special consideration.

Life isn't and will never be fair:

Thomas Sowell "As just one example, a young woman of unusual

beauty may gain many things, both personal and material, from her

looks, without having to develop other aspects of her mind and

character. Yet when age begins to rob her of that beauty, she may be

left much less able to cope then others who never had the benefit of

her earlier windfall gain. The challenge of determining the net

balance of numerous windfall advantages and disadvantages for one

individual at one given time is sufficiently daunting. To attempt the

same for whole broad brush categories of people, each in different

stages of their individual life cycles, in a complex and changing

society, suggests hubris." Wikipedia (yes, I donate to them) "Hubris -

noun: excessive pride or self-confidence. Synonyms: arrogance,

conceit, pride, superiority. I know that I am not supposed to quote

them but I really love their concept.

Summary

Nobody that I know is benefitting from things the way they are. I love people. Let's get together on some of this stuff. If we can get one of our major systems going in the right direction we will be way better off! "We must saturate every segment of American life with the realization that there is something radically wrong with the foundations of our civilization, that we must do first things first. We must get our message across to science so that they leave trips to the moon for later. First give us healthy hamburgers." - J. I. Rodale, May 1952

We have turned ourselves inside out for years and spent billions in development costs to produce fake food that replaces real food that we have plenty of. Where will our decadence end? Can we turn criminals into organic farmers? Would that really help? We need to start taking some steps in the right direction.

How do you eat an elephant?

One   bite   at   a   time.

8 STRANGE IDEAS THAT NEED TO BE OUT OF MY HEAD

Ideas that want out of my head:

Floor coating that is glow-in-the-dark and fluorescent when wet. No one pays attention to those wet floor signs. Applications - hospitals, grocery stores and retirement communities.

A tube of clothes to take on vacation that pulls out like cleaning wipes. You throw them in a bag after wearing them and return them for washing and repacking. Saves on picking, packing and storing clothes. You have to wear whatever pops out next.

Send-a-song. I often hear a song and want to send it to someone. Many times it is a song that I have already purchased from Amazon. Can I send it for a small fee and have it work for them for a period of time? Permanently? Why? to cheer, motivate, commiserate, love...

Since we can now grow kidneys in the lab, can we please grow or 3D print replacement teeth for adults? Will we all have in-home labs growing replacement parts soon?

I researched and tried for over ten years to get small wind turbines put next to highways. If you look at the grass and weeds by the road they are all bent down away from the road. I think there is some serious wind there (however turbulent). I first thought of this hearing my brother talk about people trying to drive close to police officers giving out speeding tickets to spin their hats. How much of a jerk would do that to a cop?

If you've ever changed a tire on the side of the road - you have felt the energy first hand.

I would also like to put sets of four small turbines on existing big power polls. Everything you need is right there. You could feed energy into the grid at every pole. Most of them in Michigan are already in a sort-of wind tunnel formed by the trees on either side of the power lines.

It seems like there will be a decent market for a system that re-creates body growing conditions for replacement parts in the lab. Can we use the extra heat from data centers to maintain body temperature for these "Parts Farms(TM)"?

I want a button for my steering wheel that records ideas or shopping lists that will have two buttons: record and send. I just want it to convert my talking to text and send it to my phone. I have tried to write and drive more often then I would like to admit. Finding an app on my phone while driving is ridiculous.

This one is really weird. Just go with me for a moment. Our guts and the soil of our Earth are our only sources of nutrients. We are fundamentally connected to the soil and each other. We are made to feel good when we help each other. What if what is missing from our industrial food system is that connection to healthy soil through healthy plants. We are constantly bathed in stardust. How does that influence our guts and the Earth? I want to figure out what our gut garden is supposed to look like. What if we are supposed to have forest in some places and desert in other sections of our intestines? What if depression is just a signal that a section of swamp has formed where there is supposed to be forest in our guts? Are there clues we should be picking up on to heal ourselves? Fascinating! I want to go figure this stuff out! Poop transplants are healing many conditions. Gross yes but if you feel healthy and happy after isn't it worth it? Are there poo types like blood types? Do we need to type and match? It would be so great if this is the ticket to make many, many people feel better!

Ok, we need to address the "Silent killer" uterine cancer. Are you fucking kidding? We chicks collect evidence every month! Please make a machine we can throw our pads, tampons and other items through to screen for cancer cells! Women are people too! Our bodies are more amazing then men's but they are not significantly studied. We have only been testing drugs on them for a few years! We are not slightly different from men; we are completely different in terms of our micro-biome and chemistry! What if part of what we are shedding every month are tumors? Wouldn't you want to know how we are doing that?

There are many large newspaper printing presses in the U.S. Subscriptions are down of daily papers. How fun would it be to have a real size newspaper for your homeowners association or school? My association currently prints out 3 pages, staples them together and sticks a sticker on each one for 1200 people. They then have to pay postage and mail them. Yes the info is online but it's not the same. A print run four times a year and one person to drive around has to be cheaper! How poetic is it for the local people to really take control of the press?

9 BOOKS USED

The Quest for Cosmic Justice by Thomas Sowell

Do Fathers Matter? By Paul Raeburn

Men on Strike by Helen Smith

Atlas Shrugged by Ayn Rand

The Fountainhead by Ayn Rand

Transforming a Rape Culture by Emilie Buchwald

Do Fathers Matter? - Paul Rauburn

The Way of Men - Jack Donavan

Other great sources:

 Bloomberg Business Week

 Mother Earth News

 Manosphere.co

ABOUT THE AUTHOR

Kind of a bitch but actually shy, no conflict management skills, ok friend, bad sister, BS degree that cost me multiple rapes among other things, I love helping people and am exceptionally kind to my patients, baboon-like social skills, good listener, always trying to impress people with how smart I am, pretty messy, painter and excellent at stained glass. I passionately hate to see people unhappy because they live in fear. It's unlikely that I will matter in the larger scheme of things so why be so scared?